CONTENTS

CHAPTER I

THE DAY BEFORE CHRISTMAS

The Blairs were a particularly nice family. That is what the neighbors always said of them, and, to tell the truth, the Blairs believed it. That is, the father and mother thought the children were particularly nice, and the children thought their father and mother and each other particularly nice; and so, of course, they all must have been very nice indeed.

Saturdays and Sundays and vacation days were all holidays to them, and they did such interesting things, and laughed so much as they did them, that everybody said, "What good times those Blairs do have!"

Jack and Mildred Blair were named after their father and mother, and Brownie, whose real name was Katharine, was named for her grandmother; so to avoid getting everybody mixed, the children were called the Junior Blairs by everybody.

Now it happened that there were ever so many uncles and aunts and cousins who were Blairs, too, but most of them lived a long way off, and they were very seldom able to get together for a family party; but this winter, ten of them were coming to spend Christmas with the real Blairs, and, as five of them were between fourteen and twelve, the ages of Mildred and Jack, and some more about nine, like Brownie, they were all planning to have the very nicest sort of a time, and everybody was as excited as could be.

Christmas was only two days away, when, suddenly, it began to snow. And how it snowed! The flakes came down steadily hour after hour, and soon the sidewalks were covered, and the steps were buried, and the piles of snow almost covered the gate. Everybody said that all the trains were delayed; and it was not long before the little Blairs began to whisper, "Whatever shall we do if they can't get here in time for Christmas?" Mother Blair guessed what the trouble was, and said cheerfully that, of course, the snow would stop falling before long, and the trains would be on time in the morning.

"And a beautiful white Christmas is the loveliest thing in the world," she added. But the children looked out of the window and were afraid, deep down in their hearts, that something dreadful might happen.

"If we only had something nice to do right now," groaned Jack, "so we could forget the snow. But we can't trim the tree till everybody comes to help, and the presents are all tied up, and there isn't anything Christmasy to do that *I* can think of."

"Why not cook?" suggested Mother Blair, "There are lots of things to make —Christmas things, you know."

Mildred began to brighten up. "If we could cook things all alone, I'd like that," she said.

"Boys don't cook," Jack said scornfully, still looking out of the window.

"Boys make pop-corn, though," laughed his mother. "And then suppose you make that up into nice balls, and have them all ready when the cousins come. And, Mildred, I think Norah would give you and Brownie one corner of the kitchen, and let you cook all by yourselves."

So Jack took the corn-popper and went down to the furnace, and when he opened the door, he found a great bed of red coals waiting for him; and Mildred and Brownie put on their big gingham aprons and went out into the kitchen.

The Christmas cakes

Underneath the large table was a smaller one; this Mother Blair pulled out and pushed across the room to an empty place. Then she wrote out very plainly a little receipt, and under this she explained exactly how to put things together; this she pinned on the wall over the table. "There!" she said. "Now you can go right to work." This was what was on the paper:

CHRISTMAS CAKES

¼ cup of butter.

½ cup of sugar.

¼ cup of milk.

1 egg.

1 cup of flour.

1 teaspoonful of baking-powder.

½ teaspoonful of vanilla.

Put the butter and sugar in a bowl, and rub them together till smooth and creamy. Beat the egg without separating it, and put that in next; beat all together, then add the milk, a little at a time. Put a rounded spoonful of baking-powder in the flour and stir it well, and add that slowly, mixing as you do it; and, last, put in the vanilla. Grease some little scalloped tins, and fill them half full; bake till brown.

Mildred rubbed the butter and sugar while Brownie beat the egg; they took turns putting in the other things, and, last, Norah set the tins in the oven for them. Then the two girls rushed into the sitting-room and said, "That's all done, Mother Blair! Now something else to cook, please!"

"But don't forget to watch your cakes," said Mother Blair, as she handed them a second receipt. "Open the oven door every little while just enough to peek in at them; if you forget them, they will surely burn."

The second receipt was for

OATMEAL MACAROONS

3 cups of rolled oats.

2½ teaspoonfuls of baking-powder.

½ teaspoonful of salt.

3 level tablespoonfuls of butter.

1 cup of sugar.

3 eggs, beaten separately.

1 teaspoonful of vanilla.

Put the butter and sugar in a bowl and cream them; beat the yolks of the eggs, put them in, and beat again; mix the oatmeal with the baking-powder and salt, and add this next, a little at a time; then put in the vanilla, and, last, the stiff whites of the eggs. Have ready a shallow pan, greased, and drop the batter on this in tiny bits, no larger than the end of your thumb, and two inches apart. Bake in an oven that is not very hot. When they are brown on the edges, they are done; remove them from the pan while they are still warm.

While Mildred was mixing these, Brownie took a last peep into the oven, and found the cakes were baked. Norah helped her take them out, and she herself took them from the pans and put them on a platter to cool. Then it was not long before the first panful of macaroons was done, too, and these came out all crisp and delicious.

Just as they were finishing them, their mother came out into the kitchen. "Oh, how lovely!" she exclaimed, "I never, never saw anything so good as those macaroons. Perfectly delicious!"

"But see the scalloped cakes, Mother," said Brownie. "Aren't they lovely, too?"

"Lovely? Of course they are. And I've such a bright idea about those cakes, too!"

"Oh, what?" cried both the girls together, because Mother Blair's bright ideas were always particularly nice, just like herself.

"I've been looking over the boxes of Christmas candy, and I find we have lots of candied cherries. And, Norah, you had some of the citron left from the plum-pudding, hadn't you?"

Norah said she had a large piece put away.

"Well, then, suppose we cut the citron into thin slices, and cut those up into little bits of green leaves, and cut some of the cherries into tiny bits to look like berries; then we will ice the little cakes and around each one, right on top, we will make a green holly wreath with holly berries in it. Won't those be pretty?"

"Oh, Mother, let me, let me!" Brownie begged.

"Very well, you make the leaves and berries, while Mildred ices the cakes," said Mother Blair.

So while Mildred mixed the icing, Brownie took some small scissors and cut up the citron and the cherries. At first her scissors bothered her by getting sticky, but Norah showed her how to dip them in water often and wipe them dry, and after she tried that way, she had no trouble.

Mildred's rule for icing was this:

ICING

The white of one egg.
1 teaspoonful of cold water.
1 cup of powdered sugar.
½ teaspoonful of flavoring.

Put the white of the egg in a bowl, add the water, and beat till light; stir in the sifted sugar and the flavoring, and spread on the cakes while they are still a little warm; smooth over with the blade of a knife.

After the cakes were iced, the leaves were laid in a wreath around the edges, with the tiny red berries among them; and they were the prettiest things for Christmas anybody ever saw.

When, at last, they were put away, Norah told them she had some bits of pie-crust left over from her mince-pies that they could have, if they wanted it. Brownie dashed into the hall, shouting, "Mother, Mother! What can we make with pie-crust? Norah says we can have some."

"Tartlets," called Mother Blair from upstairs. And when Brownie ran up for it she gave her this receipt:

TARTLETS

Flour the pastry board; roll out some pie-crust very thin, and press it into little scalloped tins; prick holes in the bottom to let the air in. Cut off the edges smoothly, and bake till light brown. Just before you need them fill the shells with jelly.

The very moment when the tarts disappeared in the pantry, Jack came up with his pans of pop-corn.

"Real cooking is just for girls," he said, with his mouth full of a stolen macaroon. "It's all right for boys to make pop-corn balls, though. Only how do you do it?" His mother told him to wash his hands well, and then gave him this rule:

POP-CORN BALLS

1 cup of molasses.
½ cup of sugar.
2 teaspoonfuls of vinegar.
½ teaspoonful of soda.
2 teaspoonfuls of butter.

Boil fifteen minutes, stirring all the time. Pour a little over a pan of corn, and take up in your hands all that sticks together, and roll it into a ball. Keep the candy hot on the back of the stove, and pour on more till it is all done.

This made a great dishful of lovely balls, and they set them away in a cold place; and then Norah told them they must run out of the kitchen, because she wanted to get luncheon ready.

After lunch, Jack had to go and shovel out paths again, because those he had made had all disappeared. Mildred and Brownie dressed a tiny doll for a cousin they were afraid might not have quite as many as she would want, and when that was done, they said they wanted to cook some more.

Their mother told them she had one very, very nice receipt meant especially for holidays, which, strangely enough, had Brownie's name. "Because you are so very, very nice yourself," she said with a hug, "perhaps you can make these all by yourself, too."

BROWNIES

3 squares of chocolate.

2 eggs, beaten together.

½ cup of flour.

2 cups of sugar.

¼ cup of butter.

1 cup of chopped English walnuts.

Cream the butter and sugar together, and add the eggs, well beaten without separating; then add the flour. Melt the chocolate by cutting it up into small bits and putting it in a little dish over the steam of the tea-kettle. Put this in next, and, last, the nuts. Lay a greased paper on the bottom of a shallow pan, and pour the cake in, in a thin layer. Bake twenty-five minutes; mark off into squares while warm, and cut before removing from the pan. These should be as thick as cookies when done.

"Don't you want me to help you make them, Brownie?" Mildred asked, as she read the receipt over. "You see, I could beat the eggs for you, and you know how hard it is for you not to tip the bowl over when you beat them!"

"Well," Brownie said slowly, "I might let you do just that one thing, Mildred, but Mother *said* I was to make these cakes all alone."

"But let me help just a tiny little bit," Mildred coaxed; "they do sound so interesting!"

So in the end the two made the cakes together, all delicious, and just the thing for company.

While they were still fresh from the oven, in came a pretty grown-up neighbor, whom all the Blairs, big and little, loved very much, because she always was ready for a good time with them.

"Fee-fy-fo-fum!" she exclaimed, wrinkling up her little nose. "I smell something good to eat!"

"Oh, *dear* Miss Betty," Brownie cried, "it is Christmas cooking! Come and see it."

So Miss Betty saw all the lovely little holly cakes, and the tartlets, and the macaroons, and the Brownies, and ate little crumbs off wherever she could find one. Then she said, "I want to cook too! May I, Norah?"

"Sure you may," said Norah, who thought Miss Betty was the nicest young lady in the world.

Then Miss Betty wrote out this receipt, and pinned it up, and everybody helped her make:

GINGERBREAD MEN

2 cups of molasses.
1 cup of equal parts of butter and lard, mixed.
1 level tablespoonful of ginger.
1 teaspoonful of soda.
Flour to mix very stiff.

Melt the butter, add the molasses and ginger, then the soda, dissolved in a teaspoonful of boiling water; stir in flour till the dough is so stiff you cannot stir it with a spoon; take it out on the floured board, and roll a little at a time, and with a knife cut out a man; press currants in for eyes and for buttons on his coat. Bake in a floured pan.

Gingerbread man

"These are going to be Santa Clauses," said Miss Betty. "Jack, if you will cut me some tiny cedar twigs, we will stick them in the right hands—one in each." So Jack whittled down the ends of some little twigs till they were very sharp, and while the men were warm and soft, they put a twig in the right hand of each, and they were as funny as could be.

"Now, Jack, I've something lovely for you to make!" said Miss Betty. "I came over on purpose to tell you about it."

"Boys don't cook!" said Jack, loftily.

"Boys would be perfectly wild to make these," laughed Miss Betty, "if only they knew how; but of course if you don't care to—"

"What are they?"

"Christmas elves, and the cunningest things you ever saw." She opened a box and showed them a dear, droll little figure, brown and fat. It made the children laugh to look at him.

"We will make one for each person at the Christmas dinner, and stand them at the plates with cards in the hands, to show where everybody is to sit. Now, Jack, do you want to try?"

Jack instantly was hard at work.

CHRISTMAS ELVES

Take a square of thin wood and drive two long, slender nails through it; these are the legs of the elf. Turn it upside down and push two large raisins on each nail, and then a fig on both— these are the legs and the body. Take a wire about four inches long, and put two raisins on each end, twisting up the ends to hold them. Lay this across the fig body and press it down to hold it firm. Put a marshmallow on a wooden toothpick, and put that on top for a head, and half of a fig for a cap. Draw eyes, nose, and mouth on the face with pen and ink, and, if you choose, brush a little melted chocolate on the sides of his head, for hair. Put a sprig of Christmas green in his cap.

The Christmas elves

Just as the elves were put in a row on the table. Miss Betty exclaimed, "Children, it's stopped snowing! It will be all clear to-morrow, and everybody will get here in time, after all!"

They rushed to the window to look, for sure enough, the storm was over, and everybody was going to have *AMerryChristmas* !

CHAPTER II

SUPPER AT THE HOUSE IN THE WOODS

When the Junior Blairs came down to breakfast on New Year's morning, there were three good-sized red-covered books lying on the table, one by each plate, and on the cover of each, in gold letters, was the name of Mildred, or Jack, or Brownie. But when they opened them there was nothing inside—only just white paper leaves.

"What are they for?" asked Mildred, puzzled. "For school, for examples and compositions?"

"Not a bit of it!" laughed her mother. "They are cook-books, or they will be when you have filled them full of receipts. When you made such delicious things for Christmas, I ordered these for you, so you could write down each rule that you used then, and add others as you learned other things. You see, there are little letters all down the edges of the book, and when you want to find gingerbread, for instance, all you have to do is to turn to G; and when you want—"

"Cake," interrupted Brownie, "you turn to K."

Everybody laughed then, but in a minute Jack said soberly: "If you don't mind, Mother, I think I'll use mine for school. You see, boys don't cook."

"It seems to me I've heard that before," said Father Blair, nodding at him. "But you just tuck that book away in your bureau drawer and keep it, because I've an idea you may want it yet for a cook-book."

Jack shook his head energetically, but as Norah just then brought in a fresh plate of popovers, he was too busy to say anything more.

That afternoon, the girls began their books by copying very neatly the receipts they had already used: Brownies, Christmas Cakes, Icing, Christmas Elves, Gingerbread Men, Oatmeal Macaroons, Pop-corn Balls, and Tartlets all went in, each under its own initial. Then they said they wanted some more receipts right away, because these looked so lonely.

"Very well," said their mother; "but first we will have a talk, because I have a bright idea."

Now it happened that one of the particularly nice things about the Blair family was that they owned a little bit of a house not many miles from town, right in the midst of a pine grove. A farmer lived quite close by, but the trees hid his house from sight; and the trolley-cars ran just around the corner, but they could not be seen either; so when the family went there for a day or two, or a week or two, it was just as though they were a long, long distance from everybody in the world. They called this little place the House in the Woods, and Brownie Blair often pretended it was the one in the fairy book, and that Goldilocks might come in at any moment to eat a bowl of porridge with the three Blairs, instead of the three bears.

"You see," Mother Blair went on, "the snow is still so fresh and lovely, and the sleighing so good, and the full moon is still coming up so very early, that I thought—"

"Oh, I know!" Jack shouted. "A sleighing party!"

"Yes," said his mother; "to the House in the Woods for supper. Won't that be fun? And you can cook the supper. Only, if you invite seven boys and girls to go with you, we must have plenty of things for them to eat; and of course you will want to cook them all yourselves."

"Of course," Mildred said decidedly. "What shall we have for the supper?"

"Oh, have cheese dreams!" Jack begged. "The fellows think they're great. I'll make 'em myself, if you will. I learned how at the Dwights when I was there last week."

"You did!" teased his mother. "But I thought boys didn't cook!" Jack's face grew decidedly red.

"Of course boys cook with a chafing-dish," he explained; "so do men, too. In college, lots of them make Welsh-rabbit and oysters and things like that for spreads, you know. And you can make the same things in a frying-pan on the stove just as well. So I'll make the dreams up before we go, and cook 'em when we get there."

"Very well," said his mother; "but I bargain with you that you are to put the receipt in your own cook-book." And Jack had to promise.

Then Mildred and her mother planned the rest of the supper. They were to have oyster stew, because that was what everybody wanted at a sleighing party; and then the cheese dreams, and potatoes, and cocoa; and Mother Blair said they would have a dish of scrambled eggs for anybody who did not like cheese. And, last of all, they would have little hot brown biscuits and honey; Farmer Dunn always had beautiful honey.

"Now, let us plan things out," said Mildred. "You and Brownie and I, Mother, can go out to the House in the Woods by trolley, and get the fires going and the table all ready; and Father and Jack can drive out with the others just at supper-time, and then we can all go back together afterward." This seemed the very best way of managing; so early one Saturday afternoon they reached the little house, and while Mildred and her mother went in and opened the windows and looked all around to see if everything was as they left it, Brownie ran off for Farmer Dunn, who soon brought wood and made up rousing fires in the rooms. By the time the baskets were unpacked on the kitchen table, he was ready to go back to his house and get milk and cream and eggs and butter and honey. As the Blairs always left the house ready to open at a moment's notice, they had sugar and flour and salt and things like that in the pantry.

Mildred and Brownie laid the table, putting on plates and cups and glasses, and they rubbed the forks and spoons and made them as bright as the sunshine. When it was all done, they got a beautiful great bunch of feathery pine branches for a centerpiece, and then it looked exactly as though the table knew there was going to be a party.

"It is nearly five o'clock," their mother called to them as they finished. "It is time we began to get supper. Brownie, here is a receipt for you; do you think you can manage it all alone?"

"Of course," said Brownie, with great dignity. "Only you might just tell me how, first."

Mother Blair laughed, and read the receipt over to her, and told her what to do.

STUFFED BAKED POTATOES

Take six large potatoes, wash and scrub them well, and bake them for about forty minutes in a hot oven, or till they are done. Take one potato at a time, hold it in a towel, and cut it in two, lengthwise. Scoop out the inside with a spoon into a hot bowl. When all six are ready, add ½ teaspoonful of salt and 1 teaspoonful of butter, beating and mashing well till they are light; then fill the potato shells, heaping them full; arrange in a shallow pan, and set it in the oven; bake about ten minutes, or till they are brown.

As soon as Brownie was busy with the potatoes, Mildred said she would make the cocoa, because that could stand and wait while other things cooked. Her mother told her to get the double boiler, put some hot water in the outside, and set it on the stove. Then she gave her this receipt:

COCOA

6 teaspoonfuls of cocoa.
1½ cups of boiling water.
1½ cups of boiling milk.
1 tablespoonful of powdered sugar.
1 small pinch of salt.

Always measure spoonfuls just a little rounded. Put the powdered cocoa into the double boiler and pour on it the boiling water, a little at first, stirring it until it melts; add the boiling milk, and cook two minutes, stirring all the time; add the sugar, stir a moment longer; add the salt and take from the fire. If not to be used at once, stand the double boiler on the back of the stove till wanted.

"But, Mother, we will need a great many more cups of cocoa than this," Mildred exclaimed, as she read the rule over. "Those boys will drink at least two apiece, and the girls may, too; they will all be just starving!"

"Of course," said Mother Blair. "But what do you go to school for, if not to learn multiplication? How many times over must you make the rule?"

Mildred thought two whole minutes, and then said she thought about five times would do; so she very carefully measured everything five times over. "I never thought arithmetic was any good before," she said soberly. "But now I see it is to cook by."

"Yes, I find it useful myself," her mother said, with a smile. "Now, Mildred, we might make the biscuits. I think those will not be hurt by standing any more than the cocoa will. But this rule I think you will have to multiply by three."

BAKING-POWDER BISCUITS

1 pint of sifted flour.
½ teaspoonful of salt.
4 teaspoonfuls of baking-powder.
¾ cup of milk.
1 tablespoonful of butter.

Put the salt and baking-powder in the flour and rub the butter into these with a spoon; little by little add the milk, mixing all the time; lift the dough out on the floured board, dust it over with flour, and flour the rolling-pin; roll out lightly, just once, till it is an inch thick. Flour your hands and make it into little balls as quickly as you can; put a very little flour on the bottom of a shallow pan, and put the biscuits in it, close together. Bake in a hot oven about twenty minutes, or till they are brown.

These were great fun to make, and when the very last panful was done, Mildred tucked all the little brown biscuits up in a big fresh towel, and put them in a pan in the warming oven to keep hot till they were needed. At that very minute, they heard sleigh-bells, and everybody rushed to throw open the door and let the party in. Such shouting and laughing and talking you never heard in all your life! All the boys and girls had been out to the House in the Woods often before, and they were so glad to come again, they hardly knew what to do.

While they were taking off their wraps, Jack slipped out into the kitchen and demanded the frying-pan. "See," he said proudly, opening a box, "here are the cheese dreams, all ready to cook! Aren't they fine?"

"Lovely!" exclaimed his mother, and then added, with a merry twinkle in her eyes, "you'll be a great cook yet, Jack!"

This was the receipt Jack had used to make them:

CHEESE DREAMS

(Six large sandwiches)

12 slices of bread, cut half an inch thick.
12 thin slices of cheese.
1 pinch of soda, cayenne pepper, and salt for each slice.

Put together like sandwiches, and then cut into rounds. Heat a frying-pan very hot, melt a teaspoonful of butter in it, and lay in two or three sandwiches; when one side is brown, turn it over and cook the other; take from the pan and lay in the oven in a pan on a paper till all are ready.

Jack Fried the "Cheese Dreams"

Of course Jack had made more than six sandwiches, for he knew everybody would want two apiece; so he had a great boxful, and it took him quite a little time to fry them all; but it was just as well, for Mildred and her mother had to make the oyster stew, which was to be eaten first.

OYSTER STEW

1 pint of oysters.
½ pint of water.
1 quart of rich milk.
½ teaspoonful of salt.

Drain the juice off the oysters and examine each to remove any pieces of shell that may still adhere to it; add the water to the oyster juice, and boil one minute; skim this well. Heat the milk and add to this, and when it steams, drop in the oysters and simmer just one minute, or till the edges of the oysters begin to curl; add the salt and take up at once; if you choose, add a cup of sifted cracker crumbs.

"What is 'simmer?'" asked Mildred, as she read the rule over.

"Just letting it boil a tiny little bit," said her mother, "around the edges of the saucepan, but not all over. And here is the receipt for:"

SCRAMBLED EGGS

1 egg for each person.
2 tablespoonfuls of milk to each egg.
2 shakes of salt.
1 shake of pepper.

Break the eggs in a bowl, beat them twelve times, then add the milk, salt, and pepper; heat a pan, put in a piece of butter the size of a hickory-nut, and when it is melted, pour in the eggs; stir them as they cook, and scrape them off the bottom of the pan; when they are all thick and creamy, they are done.

"I have taken the rule for the stew three times over for twelve people, and I don't think it will be a bit too much; but as almost everyone will want the cheese dreams, suppose we scramble only five eggs.

"You'd better do that right away, for supper is almost ready. Brownie's potatoes are just done, and she can be filling the glasses with water, and putting on the butter and bread, and these two big dishes of honey to eat with the biscuits for the last course."

While Mildred was cooking the eggs, Mother Blair put the oysters on the table, with the hot soup-plates and a generous supply of crisp oyster-crackers; the cheese dreams were done and in the oven, and Mildred covered the eggs and set the dish in the warming oven, and put the cocoa on the table in a chocolate pot. Then everybody sat down and began to eat.

After the oyster stew was all gone, they had the hot cheese dreams and scrambled eggs and the stuffed potatoes and cocoa all at once; and when those too had vanished, there were the little biscuits and the beautiful golden clover-honey in the comb, and perhaps that was the very best of all.

"Never, never, did I eat anything so good as this supper!" Father Blair said solemnly, as he ate his fourth biscuit. "That oyster stew—those potatoes—

the cheese dreams—"

"What a greedy father!" said Mildred. "And you never said a word about the cocoa—"

"Nor about the scrambled eggs—" said Brownie, eagerly.

"But I ate them all," said her father. "I ate everything I was given, and I should like to eat them all again! Next time we come, have twice as much of everything, won't you?"

But everybody else said that they couldn't have eaten one single crumb more. And they knew perfectly well that Father Blair couldn't, either.

Then everybody helped wash the dishes and put things away, and Farmer Dunn came over to put out the fires and shut the doors; and presently it was all dark in the House in the Woods, and so still that, far, far off, you could hear the sound of the singing of the boys and girls as they rode home across the snow.

CHAPTER III

JACK'S SCHOOL-LUNCHEONS

"Mother," said Jack, one evening, "I'd like to take my lunch to school for the next few weeks; all the fellows are going to, so we can have more time for class elections and so on. Do you suppose Norah could put up one for me every morning?"

"Why not let Mildred put it up? Her school is so near that she does not have to start till long after you do; and then, Jack, you could easily pay her for her trouble by helping her with her Latin; you know she is bothered with that just now."

Mildred was overjoyed at the suggestion of the bargain. "Oh, Jack! I'll do you up the most beautiful luncheons in the world if you will only help me with that horrid Cæsar. I'm just as stupid as I can be about it. What do you like best to eat in all the world?"

Jack said he wasn't very particular as long as he had plenty of pie and cake and pickles and pudding and ice-cream; Mildred laughed, and said she guessed she could manage to think up a few other things beside.

So the very next morning she put up the first luncheon. But, alas, Norah had no cold meat to slice—only bits of beefsteak left from dinner; and not a single piece of cake. All she could find for lunch was some plain bread and butter, which she cut rather thick, a hard-boiled egg, and an apple. "Pretty poor," she sighed, as she saw him trudge off with the box under his arm.

That afternoon, when she came home from school, she went to Mother Blair for help. "I must give him nice luncheons," she explained. "Now what can I have for to-morrow? I can't think of anything at all, except bread and cake, and stupid things like those."

"Oh, there are lots and lots of things," said her mother. "Putting up lunches is just fun! I only wish you would do up some for me, too! And first, dear, you had better see that there is plenty of bread, because it takes a good deal for sandwiches, and it must not be too fresh to slice nicely, nor too stale; day-old bread is best. And if you can find some brown bread as well as white, that will be ever so nice. You will want cake, too, and fruit; you might ask Norah what she has on hand."

In a moment, Mildred came back with the news that, as there was to be fish for dinner, there would be no left-over meat at all in the morning; the bits of steak were still there. "But imagine beefsteak sandwiches!" said she, scornfully. And though there was no cake now, Norah was going to make some.

"I think we had better learn first how to make all kinds of sandwiches, because that will help you more than anything else in putting up lunches," her mother said, getting out her cook-book. "You will need some paraffin paper for them, too, and paper napkins; suppose you look on the top shelf of the kitchen closet and see if we had any left over from summer picnics."

By the time Mildred had found these, as well as a box to pack the lunch in, these receipts were all ready for her to copy in her own book:

SANDWICHES

Use bread that is at least a day old. Spread the butter smoothly on the loaf; if it is too cold to spread well, warm it a little; slice thin, with a sharp knife; spread one slice with the filling, lay on another, press together, and trim off the heavy part of the crust; cut in two pieces, or, if the slices are very large, in three. Put two or three sandwiches of the same kind together, and wrap in paraffin paper.

MEAT SANDWICHES

Take any cold meat, cut off the gristle and fat, and put it through the meat chopper. Add a pinch of salt, a pinch of dry mustard, a shake of pepper, and, last, a teaspoonful of melted butter; press into a cup, and put away to grow firm.

"Now you see the nice thing about this rule is, that any sort of cold meat will do to use, and if you have bits of two or more kinds, you can use them together. There are those beefsteak ends; all you have to do is to follow your rule, and they will make as good sandwiches as anything else."

"But, Mother, if you had nice roast-beef slices, you would not chop those up, would you?"

"No, indeed! I would make sandwiches of plain bread and butter and put the slices of meat in by themselves. But chopped meat makes better sandwiches than slices of meat between bread."

"But what do you make sandwiches out of if you don't use meat? I think plain bread and butter is horrid for lunches."

"Oh, there are plenty of other things to use; see, here are your next rules:"

EGG SANDWICHES

1 hard-boiled egg, chopped fine.
1 teaspoonful of oil.
3 drops of vinegar.

1 pinch of salt.

1 shake of pepper.

Mix well and spread on buttered bread.

"And then sometimes you can have:"

CHEESE SANDWICHES

Spread thin buttered brown bread with cream cheese; sprinkle with a very little salt and pepper. Sometimes add chopped nuts for a change.

"Or, here are these:"

LETTUCE SANDWICHES

Spread some very thin white bread; lay on a leaf of lettuce; sprinkle with a very little oil, vinegar, salt, and pepper, as in the egg sandwiches.

SARDINE SANDWICHES

Drain off all the oil from a little tin of sardines; skin each fish, take out the bones, and mash smoothly, adding a teaspoonful of lemon juice; spread on white buttered bread.

"And then, when you have no cake or cookies for lunch, you can have two or three sandwiches with meat and two more like these:"

SWEET SANDWICHES

Spread buttered bread with a very little jam or jelly; or with chopped dates or figs; or with scraped maple sugar; or with chopped raisins and nuts; or with a thick layer of brown sugar.

"Those are just as good as cake, and better, I think," said Mother Blair, as Mildred finished copying them all down. "And now, what comes next in a lunch, after sandwiches?"

"Cake," said Mildred, promptly.

"Yes, sometimes, but not always. What else can you think of that would be nice?"

Mildred said she thought gingerbread might be good, or perhaps doughnuts; but she could not think of anything else.

"Oh, I can think of ever so many things," said her mother. "But we will put down the gingerbread first; and, by the way, what do you think Betty calls it? This:"

"PERFECTLY LOVELY" GINGERBREAD

1 cup of molasses.
1 cup of shortening (butter and lard mixed).
3 cups of flour.
1 teaspoonful each of cloves, cinnamon, nutmeg, ginger, and soda.
1 cup of sugar.
2 eggs.
1 cup of milk.

Cream the butter and sugar, add the eggs, well beaten without separating, then the molasses mixed with the spices and soda, then the flour, then the milk. Stir and beat well. Put in a shallow tin and bake slowly.

"Things don't sound as good as they taste, do they?" said Mildred, as she read the receipt over. "I just love gingerbread, but butter and lard and soda don't sound appetizing."

"Well, then, try this," laughed Mother Blair; "every bit of this sounds good:"

PEANUT WAFERS

1 cup of sugar.

½ cup of milk.

½ teaspoonful of soda.

½ cup of butter.

2 cups of flour.

1 cup of chopped peanuts.

Cream the butter and sugar; put the soda in the milk, stir thoroughly, and put in next; then the flour. Beat well. Grease a shallow pan and spread the mixture evenly over the bottom, and scatter the nuts on top. Bake till light brown, and cut in squares while warm.

"Oh, those *do* sound good!" Mildred exclaimed, as she wrote the last words down.

Brownie and Mildred Making "Chocolate Crackers"

"What sounds good?" asked Miss Betty's voice, as her pretty head popped in the door. So they told her all about the luncheons, and she said she knew some good things, too, and the first one was:

CHOCOLATE CRACKERS

2 squares of chocolate.
1 teaspoonful of sugar.
   Butter, the size of the tip of your thumb.
3 drops of vanilla.

Cut the chocolate up into bits and put it in a saucer over the tea-kettle; when it melts, add the sugar and butter and vanilla; stir, and drop in some small crackers, only one at a time, and lay them on a greased paper to dry.

"I've got to make some this very minute."

"Oh, Mother, I've just got to stop writing and make some of those this very minute!" Mildred exclaimed. Miss Betty said she had lots of things she wanted to talk over with Mother Blair while Mildred was busy. Brownie came running in just then, and the two girls worked so fast they had a whole plateful of crackers done in no time; and after everybody had had one apiece to eat, Mildred said: "Now, I will learn to make some more things."

"Let me see," said her mother, slowly. "Sandwiches and cake—what else can you think of for luncheons, Betty?"

"Deviled eggs," said Miss Betty, as quick as a flash. "Please let me tell how!"

DEVILED EGGS

Boil three eggs for ten minutes; peel them, cut them in halves, and put the yolks in a bowl; add

¼ teaspoonful of salt.
¼ teaspoonful of dry mustard.
1 pinch of pepper.
1 teaspoonful of oil.
½ teaspoonful of vinegar.

Mix well, fill the whites, press smooth with a knife, and put two halves together.

"But three eggs are too many for Jack," complained Brownie. "He won't need three; can't I have one for my lunch here?"

Miss Betty laughed, and said it would be easy for Mildred to make enough for everybody instead of making three, as the rule said.

"If I just made one, I suppose I'd take pinches instead of teaspoonfuls," said Mildred, thoughtfully. "I mean, I'd take just a little of everything, enough to make the egg taste good?"

"Exactly!" said Miss Betty; "that is just the way a real grown-up cook does. And, Mildred, when I had to take my lunch to school, I used to have the best thing—salad. I had it when there were no real sandwiches, only bread and butter; it was put in a little round china jar with a tin top that screwed on, so it never spilled. But perhaps Jack doesn't like salad."

"He just loves it," said Brownie; "he loves every single thing to eat that there is!"

"Then he will surely 'just love' these things! Write them down, Mildred."

CHICKEN SALAD

½ cup of cold chicken, cut in small bits.
½ a hard boiled egg, cut up.

Or use celery in place of the egg, or use both.

FRENCH DRESSING

2 teaspoonfuls of oil.
¼ teaspoonful vinegar.
1 pinch of salt
2 shakes of pepper (paprika is best).

Beat the dressing well and mix with the chicken and egg.

Make more dressing if the salad is too dry.

LUNCHEON FRUIT SALAD

Cut a seedless orange in halves; take out the pulp with a spoon; use alone, or mix with bits of banana or other fruit; or use chopped celery and apple together. Add the dressing.

"There!" said Miss Betty, triumphantly, as Mildred read the receipts aloud when she had copied them. "If Jack doesn't like those, he isn't the boy I take him for. And you see, Mildred, when you have no salad for him, you can sometimes put in a nice stalk of celery; and when you have had the same fruit over and over, you can just give him a fruit salad. I do believe I'll start on a long journey and take a whole week's supply of lunches along. All these receipts make me feel just like it!"

"Oh, do let me go too," begged Mildred.

"So you shall," laughed Miss Betty. "But before we start, I must tell you one thing more: if you want an ab-so-lute-ly perfect lunch, you must always have a surprise for the very last thing of all."

"How do you make one?" asked Brownie, curiously.

"Oh, you don't make them at all, or at least not usually; a surprise is something which has to be eaten last of all, after all the sandwiches and other things are gone, for a sort of dessert; sometimes I had a piece of maple-sugar, or a bit of sweet chocolate, or a couple of marshmallows; sometimes it was a fig or two, or a few dates. But it was always hidden down in the very bottom of the box, and everything had to be finished up before I opened the little paper it was in. Honestly, I don't think boys need surprises at all, because they will eat everything up any way, but often girls will skip a sandwich or two, unless they know about the surprise."

"When I take my lunch, I shall have one every time," said Brownie.

"So shall I," laughed Mother Blair.

"I shall certainly give Jack one every day, because of Cæsar," said Mildred.

The next morning bright and early, Mildred hurried to get Jack's luncheon all ready before breakfast, and her mother said she would help her, just for once. First they made three beautiful thin sandwiches out of bread and butter spread with the nice beefsteak filling, and wrapped these up by themselves and put them in one corner of the box; then in the opposite corner went the surprise, this time four little chocolate crackers, all wrapped up carefully; on top of them, to hide them, went three more sandwiches, made of brown bread and butter and cheese; then the deviled egg filled the corner on top of the other pile, and one of Norah's cakes was put opposite.

"Now for the fruit," said Mother Blair. "What is there?"

Mildred said there was an orange, but it would not go in the box.

"Oh, you don't give anybody an orange whole for luncheon! Peel it first, then break it carefully in halves, wrap each half up in paper by itself, and you will see how well it fits in and how easy it will be to eat when you have no fruit-knife or orange-spoon to use with it. Now that is all, and it's what I call a perfectly delicious luncheon, don't you?"

"*Perfectly!*" said Mildred, rapturously, as she tied up the box. "I guess the other boys will wish they had lunches just exactly like it; and I think it's very interesting to do them up, too."

That afternoon, when Jack came home from school, he shouted up the stairs:

"Say, Mildred, what will you take to do up lunches for the crowd? They told me to ask you. They said they had never seen anything so good. Where is that Cæsar? I'll do about ten pages for you if you want me to."

When the lesson was over, Mildred hugged Jack gratefully. "I can do it alone in no time now, because you're such a good teacher," she said, as Jack squirmed away. "And, when summer comes, just think of all the picnic lunches I can do up for everybody!"

"We won't wait till summer for a picnic," said Mother Blair. "I've got *such* a bright idea!"

CHAPTER IV

THE BIRTHDAY PICNIC

Just as Mother Blair declared that she had "*such* a bright idea!" a caller came in, and it was dinner-time before Mildred had a chance to ask her what it was. And then her mother put her finger on her lip and shook her head; so Mildred knew, of course, that it was a secret, and waited till later on to hear what it was.

"Now I will tell you all about it," Mother Blair said, after she had read Brownie a fairy story and tucked her up for the night. "Jack, you can hear, too, and Father, if he wants to." So they all drew up around the fire to listen.

"You remember how much Brownie loved the picnics we had last summer," she began. "She used to say that she would rather eat plain bread and butter out of doors than ice-cream in the dining-room; and whenever we took our supper and went off for the afternoon, she was so happy!"

"So she was," said Father Blair. "Brownie is her father's own daughter; I love picnics too."

"But, Mother, we can't have a picnic at this time of year!" exclaimed Mildred. "Just listen to the rain and snow coming down together this minute; and the slush on the sidewalk is so deep you have to wade to school."

"But this is just where my bright idea comes in! You see, next week will be Brownie's birthday, and every year since she was two, she has had some sort of a party; now this year, for a real change, I think it would be fun to have a picnic for her, a lovely in-door picnic, for ten boys and girls; and we'll have it up in the attic!"

"Isn't that just like Mother!" Jack exclaimed, laughing. "Who else in the world would ever have thought of such a thing!"

"But think what fun it will be!" Mother Blair went on, her cheeks growing pink as she explained all about it. "The attic is nice and large, and empty except for the trunks and old furniture which are tucked away around the eaves. The children will all come in their every-day clothes, and wear their coats and hats, so they won't take cold up there. And we can spread down in the middle of the open space the two old green parlor carpets, for grass; they are all worn out, but nobody will notice that. And then, Jack, you can carry up the two palms and the rubber plant, and put them on the edge of the 'grass,' and Farmer Brown can bring us in some little cedar-and spruce-trees from the woods the next time he drives to town, and we will plant them in sand in big earthen flower-pots, and stand those around, too. Can't you see how lovely it will be? Just like a little grassy grove!"

Everybody laughed, but everybody thought it was going to be great fun to make a picnic-place in the attic.

"And we will tie a hammock to the rafters," said Father Blair; "and there is the old ping-pong set to play with, and the ring-toss; and the boys can play ball, if they choose; there's nothing they can hurt."

And so it was all arranged; and Brownie was told she was going to have a beautiful surprise for her birthday, and she must not ask a single question about it. Mother Blair asked ten boys and girls to come at twelve on Saturday and spend the rest of the day, and, after the notes were sent, she and Mildred began to plan the luncheon.

"Of course all the things must be packed in baskets," said Mildred, "exactly like a regular picnic."

"Of course!" said her mother. "And in one basket we will put a lunch cloth to lay on the 'grass,' and wooden plates, and paper napkins, and glasses, and forks. And they can spread the cloth and arrange everything themselves."

"And what will they have to eat? They are sure to be dreadfully hungry."

"Well, there must be one substantial dish to begin with. We might have cold sliced ham, of course, but I think perhaps they would like something else better. Suppose we have veal loaf?"

"Just the very thing," said Mildred. "May I make it?"

"Of course you may, and everything else as well, if you want to. If you will get your book, you can write down the receipts this minute. Here is the first:"

VEAL LOAF

2 pounds of veal, chopped fine.
¼ pound of salt pork, chopped with it.
½ cup of bread crumbs, soaked in milk.
1 egg.
1 teaspoonful of chopped onion.
½ teaspoonful each of pepper and paprika.
1 level teaspoonful of salt.

Have the meats chopped together at the market; put the crumbs in a bowl and cover them with milk, and let them stand for fifteen minutes; then squeeze them dry and add to the meat. Beat the egg without separating it, and mix that in next, and then the seasoning. Stir all together, and put in a bread tin and bake one hour. Have on the stove a cup half full of hot water mixed with two tablespoonfuls of butter, and every fifteen minutes open the oven door and pour a quarter of this over the meat. When done, put in a cold place over night. Slice thin, and put parsley around it.

"You see, this is very easy to make, and it is always good for luncheon for ourselves, and for Sunday night supper as well. You can make it Friday afternoon, and then, by the time for the picnic, it will be ready to slice."

"And what are they to eat with it?"

"I think it would be nice to have some sandwiches—hot ones."

"Hot sandwiches, Mother Blair! I never heard of them. How do you make them?"

"I invented them myself," laughed her mother. "I really did, this very morning, when I was thinking about the picnic. Here is the rule."

TOASTED SARDINE SANDWICHES

1 tin sardines.

8 slices of toast.

½ a lemon.

Large pinch of salt, and as much dry mustard.

Open a can of sardines, drain off the oil, and spread them on brown paper. Scrape off the skin carefully, and open each one on the side and take out the back bone. Sprinkle over them all the salt and mustard, and squeeze the lemon on. Then make the toast, large brown slices, and butter them a little; lay two together, trim off the crust, and cut them in strips. Open the strips, and between each two put one sardine and press together. Put them in the oven between two hot plates till needed.

"Oh, those do sound *so* good! Can't I make some for lunch to-day, Mother?" Mildred begged.

"But they belong to the surprise! Let's wait till after the picnic, and then you may make lots of them."

"Well!" sighed Mildred, "then let me have another receipt right away, so I'll forget them. I do want to make them so much."

"Here is another receipt you will like just as well; part of it is for the picnic, and part of it is for a little bit of a party for you and Miss Betty and me, while the picnic is going on upstairs."

"A party for us? What kind of a party?"

"Lovely grown-up afternoon tea!" laughed her mother. "You can invite Miss Betty yourself won't that be nice?"

"*Perfectly* lovely! Do tell faster!"

"Well, first you make for the picnic some sweet sandwiches like those we planned for the school lunches; these are simply, to begin with:"

ORANGE MARMALADE SANDWICHES

Spread thin white bread and butter with orange marmalade; trim off the crusts and cut into even shapes; a round cooky cutter makes pretty sandwiches.

"I've made those for Jack, lots of times," said Mildred, as she wrote this down, "only I didn't cut them in round shapes, because boys don't care about that."

"No," said her mother, smiling, "boys don't, but girls do! So make part of these in rounds, and put them away, and send the square ones upstairs. And when it's time for our party, just toast ours quickly, and you will find them the most delicious things you ever ate, especially with tea; that's what we three will have."

"Those will be Miss Betty's surprise!" laughed Mildred, as she wrote down the word *toasted* after the title of the sandwiches. "Now what next?"

"Suppose you try some very easy cookies; those are just the thing for a picnic; you can make them Saturday morning, and then they will be fresh. Here is the rule:"

SPICY COOKIES

Sprinkle the baking board with flour and rub it smoothly over; do the same to the rolling-pin, and scatter a little flour evenly also over the bottom of some shallow tins. Have a panful of sifted flour ready on the table, as you may need to do this several times.

¾ cup of sugar.
3 tablespoonfuls of butter.
6 tablespoonfuls of milk.
1 egg.
1½ cups of flour.
¼ teaspoonful of soda.

¼ teaspoonful of salt.

1 tablespoonful of hot water.

¼ teaspoonful of cloves.

¼ teaspoonful of cinnamon.

Melt the butter, add the sugar, and rub together. Beat the egg without separating, and put in next. Mix the soda and hot water, put the milk with this; put the salt in the flour; add part of the flour to the sugar and other things, and then part of the milk, and so on; then put in the spices and stir all together. Put the dough on the board, roll it out thin, and with a cutter mark it all over; then lift out the pieces with a cake turner, very carefully, and arrange them in your pans, but do not let them touch. Bake fifteen minutes; take them out of the pans while warm, and spread out on a platter to cool.

"Dear me, that sounds pretty hard!" said Mildred, as she finished.

"Cookies are not quite as easy to make as some other things, but they are so good, so nice for luncheon and suppers and other times, that I think you will be glad to know how to make them. And Father is so fond of cookies!"

"So he is. Well, Mother, I'll try them. And now what comes next?"

"Some cunning, easy little cakes, so easy that next time Brownie can make them herself. They are called:"

MARGUERITES

20 round, thin crackers.

20 marshmallows.

2 tablespoonfuls of chopped nuts.

2 teaspoonfuls of butter.

Butter the crackers on one side, just a little; put a marshmallow on each, a tiny bit of butter on it, and a sprinkle of chopped nuts of any kind. Put them in a shallow pan, and bake till they are soft and brown; eat while fresh and warm.

"Oh, lovely! Mother, I must have some of the girls in and have those for myself!"

"So you shall, any day you want to. Now don't you think that is almost enough for the picnic?"

"I think we ought to have something to finish off with—to eat with the cookies and marguerites; don't you think so?"

"Yes, I do; something in the way of fruit. Suppose we give them this—it is much nicer than plain oranges or bananas; write it down, dear."

ORANGE BASKETS

6 large oranges.
2 bananas.
2 tablespoonfuls of powdered sugar.

Cut the oranges in halves; take out the pulp with a spoon, and put it in a bowl. Scrape out the inside, leaving nice, clean shells, and then scallop or point the edges with the scissors. Peel the bananas, cut them in long, narrow strips, and these into small bits, and mix lightly with the orange, and add the sugar; heap in the baskets and set away to grow cold.

Making "Orange Baskets"

"If we happened to have any pineapple or white grapes in the house, I should put some of those in too; but these will be delicious just as they are. Now anything more?"

"Something to drink with the lunch. I think pink lemonade would be nice."

"Perfectly lovely!" laughed Mother Blair. "We will get a can of raspberries out of the fruit closet, and make something for them that will be ever so good. This is the rule:"

PICNIC LEMONADE

8 lemons.
12 glasses of water.
3 cups of sugar.
1 cup of raspberry juice.

> Roll the lemons till they are soft; cut them and squeeze the juice out. Put the sugar in a little pan with a glass of water, and boil it two minutes; add this to the lemon and raspberry juice, and strain it; add the rest of the water; serve with broken ice in a glass pitcher.

"Be sure and boil the sugar and water together, Mildred, whenever you make any kind of drink like lemonade; it is so much better than if you put in plain sugar. When it is all done, if it is not quite sweet enough, you can add a little powdered sugar without hurting it."

"Mother, we forgot the surprise! You remember, 'every luncheon must have a surprise,' you said; see, here it is in the book."

"Dear me, so I did! What shall it be, Mildred? I can't seem to think of another thing for that picnic."

"Neither can I."

"Stuffed dates!" exclaimed Mother Blair, presently. "I knew there must be something, and those will be exactly right."

STUFFED DATES

> Wash the dates and wipe them dry. Open one side and take out the stone; in its place press in half a pecan or other nut; close the edges, and roll each date in powdered sugar.

"I do hope there will be some of those over for us," said Mildred, as she put her book away. "Those children are going to have a *wonderful* lunch!"

Brownie could not imagine what her birthday surprise was to be. She could not help guessing, but she never once was "warm." When Saturday came, and the boys and girls arrived in their every-day clothes and even kept on their wraps in the parlor, she did not know what to think; and there was actually no lunch for them in the dining-room! She began to look very sober.

But when everybody had come, Mother Blair said: "Won't you go upstairs?" and Mildred and Jack ushered them up to the attic.

It was such a lovely surprise! The big green carpets were spread down on the bare floor, and all around were set little green trees in pots. The canary was hung up out of sight, and he was singing as hard as he could. It was not a bit too cold, for the door had been kept open all day and the sun was shining in at the window.

And just then appeared Mother Blair, and Norah, and Jack, and Mildred, all carrying baskets, which they put down on the floor. Then the picnic began!

There was first the cloth to spread down on the grass, and paper plates and napkins to be passed around. The veal loaf was found, a platter of it tied up in a large napkin, and hot sandwiches between hot plates, tied up in another napkin, and marmalade sandwiches folded in paraffin paper by themselves. Last of all were the orange baskets, each one twisted up in a paper napkin with a funny little frill on top made of the ends of the napkin; and the dates were in little square paper boxes, one box for each child.

Jack and the lemonade

As they began to eat, Jack came up with a big, big pitcher of beautiful pink lemonade, and little glasses to drink it out of. Oh, such a picnic as it was! Such a perfectly lovely picnic! Out-of-door picnics were nothing to it And when they had eaten up every crumb and drank up every drop, they played games until the attic grew dark; and then they all went home, and the birthday was over.

CHAPTER V

SUNDAY NIGHT SUPPER

One Sunday afternoon just as the clock struck three, the Blairs' telephone rang; and after she had answered it, Mother Blair called Mildred, who sat reading by the window.

"My dear," she said, "do you remember hearing Father speak of his old friends the Wentworths, whom he used to know so well years ago? Well, they have come east, and are in town for a day or two, and they want to come out and see us this very afternoon. Now I should love to ask them to stay to supper, but if I do, I shall have to stay with them and visit and can't help you at all; and Norah is out. Do you suppose you three children could get the supper and serve it all by yourselves?"

"Why, of course, Mother Blair," said Mildred, reproachfully. "Of *course* we can! You don't know how many things your children can do when they try! Now what shall we have? It ought to be something very good, because they have never been here before."

"We were going to have canned salmon," said her mother, thoughtfully; "we might scallop that, and have potatoes with it, and perhaps muffins or biscuits."

"Oh, have muffins, Mother! I have seen Norah make them lots of times, and I'm sure I could, too, if you give me the receipt."

"Well, you may try," said her mother, "but I think you had better have some toast ready, too, in case they do not come out right. And what else can we have? Preserves, I suppose; but, Mildred, all the nice preserves are gone, because it is so late in the spring. But we might have little baked custards."

"Yes, in the cunning little brown baking dishes; those will be lovely! And I'll make some little cakes to eat with them; Norah said there were just cookies for supper."

"But do you really think you can do all that? Don't you think the cookies will do?"

"No, indeed," said Mildred, "not for extra nice company! But little cakes are no trouble to make. And isn't it fun to have company come when you don't expect it? It's so much nicer than to specially invite them!"

Mother Blair laughed. "I hope you will always think so," she said. And Mildred ran away to call Brownie to get her apron and come to the kitchen.

"We will lay the table first, even though it is so early," said their mother. "Brownie, bring me the pile of the best doilies in the sideboard drawer."

"The Wheelers always use a regular big cloth for supper," Brownie said, as she came over with them to the table.

"Many people do, but I think the table looks prettier at breakfast and luncheon and supper with the doilies. And then, too, if anybody happens to spill anything—"

"Jack spilled gravy yesterday, awfully," said Brownie, soberly.

"Well, you see Norah had to wash only one little doily because of that; if we had had on a table-cloth, all of it would have had to go into the wash. But if we had no doilies, I should use a lunch cloth that would just cover the top of the table, and that would be pretty, too. Put one doily for each person, Brownie, and a large one in the middle for the fern dish, and little ones for the tumblers. Now for the silver."

Mildred came with knives, forks, and spoons.

"No knives, because there is no meat," said her mother; "but if we were going to use them, which side would you put them on?"

"Left," said Brownie, guessing.

"Not unless you were left-handed," smiled her mother. "The rule is: put on the right side what you will use with the right hand, and on the left what you will use with the left hand. That is, if there are no knives, all the silver goes on the right, and the fork or spoon you are to use first goes the farthest away from the plate, the next one next to that, and so on; if you remember that, you will never be puzzled as to which fork to use. Now the teaspoons —put those on the right, too; and the dessert spoon or fork may go at the top, across the plate if you like, though I prefer it on the dessert plate itself. Put the napkin at the left, always; and the tumbler goes at the top to the right, and the bread-and-butter plate and knife at the top too, toward the left. There! Doesn't that look pretty?"

Arranging a Small Round Tray in Front of her Mother's Place

Mildred had been getting out the best cups and saucers and arranging a small round tray in front of her mother's place with cream and sugar and the tray bowl, and a place left for the tea-pot; the cups she put at the right, arranging them in twos—two cups on two saucers.

"Mildred, after you pass the salmon, you may put the dish right in front of Father; and the potatoes may go on the table too, as Norah isn't here, though I like best to have them passed from the sideboard. The muffins may stand at the side of the table, half-way down. Now let us carry out all the dishes and begin to cook."

So Mildred took a pile of plates to heat, and Brownie carried a dish for the potatoes, and Mother Blair brought the little custard cups; they arranged these on the kitchen table where they would not be in the way, and then Mother Blair told Mildred to see that the fire was all right. "Always remember to look at that first," she said. "It needs shaking down a little, and to have more coal on; and pull out the dampers so the oven will heat."

Mildred hunted for the dampers, but could not find any. "I don't believe there are any on this stove," she said, just as Jack came in to see what was going on.

"No dampers! Isn't that just like a girl!" he exclaimed. "See, here they are, tucked under the edge of the stove. You pull them out—so—and then you shut the draft at the top, opposite the coal, and open the one at the bottom, so the air will blow right up through the fire and make it go like everything. And you have to turn the dampers in the pipe, too, to let the heat go up the chimney."

"Good!" said his mother. "I didn't know you knew so much about stoves. Now suppose you shake the fire down and put the coal on—that's a man's work."

"All right," said Jack; "I don't mind things like that; but boys don't cook, you know."

His mother put both hands over her ears. "Jack, if I hear you say that once more, I shall believe you are turning into a parrot! And you are all wrong, too, and some day I am going to give you some special lessons myself. But to-day you may just tend the fire and bring us things from the refrigerator as we need them, to save time. Now, Mildred, we will begin with the custards, because they must be nice and cold. Brownie, you bring the spoons and bowls and such things, and, Jack, you get the milk and eggs."

BAKED CUSTARDS

1 quart of milk.

Yolks of four eggs.

4 teaspoonfuls of sugar.

½ teaspoonful of vanilla.

1 pinch of salt.

½ teaspoonful of grated nutmeg.

Put the sugar in the milk; beat the eggs light, and add those, with salt and vanilla. Pour into the cups, sprinkle with nutmeg, and arrange the cups in a shallow pan. Bake half an hour, or till, when you put the blade of a knife in one, it comes out clean.

It took just a few moments to make these, and then came the next rule:

CURRANT CAKES

½ cup of butter.

1 cup of sugar.

1 cup of milk.

1 egg.

2 cups of flour.

2 rounded teaspoonfuls of baking-powder.

½ cup of currants.

1 teaspoonful of vanilla.

Wash the currants and rub them dry in a towel. Put the flour in a bowl; take out a large tablespoonful and mix with the currants, and then mix the baking-powder with the rest of it. Rub the butter to a cream, add the sugar, then the milk, then the egg, beaten without separating, then the flour mixed with the baking-powder, then the flavoring, and, last, the currants. Grease some small tins, fill them half full, and bake in an oven not too hot.

"You must always mix some flour with raisins or currants to keep them from sinking to the bottom of the cake; but do not add any to the rule—just take a little out from what you are going to use in the cake. Now, Jack, please get me two cans of salmon from the pantry and open them; and we will need butter and milk from the refrigerator, too. It's fine to have a 'handy man' around to help us cook! Now, Mildred, double this rule, because there will be so many at supper."

SCALLOPED SALMON

1 good-sized can of salmon, or one pint of any cooked fish.
1 cup of white sauce.
1 cup of cracker crumbs.

Butter a baking dish, put in a layer of fish, then one of crumbs; sprinkle with a little salt and pepper, and dot the crumbs with butter; then put on a layer of white sauce. Repeat till the dish is full, with the crumbs on top; dot with butter and brown well in the oven; it will take about twenty minutes.

Brownie rolled the crackers

Brownie rolled the crackers for this, while Mildred made the white sauce by the rule she said was so easy it was exactly like learning a bc.

"That is so queer," laughed her mother, "because cooks call it just that—the a b c of cooking! It is the rule you use more often than any other."

WHITE SAUCE

1 rounded tablespoonful of butter.
1 rounded tablespoonful of flour.
1 cup of milk.
½ teaspoonful of salt.
2 shakes of pepper.

Melt the butter; when it bubbles, put in the flour, stirring it well; when this is smooth, slowly add the milk, salt, and pepper; stir and cook till very smooth; you can make it like thin cream by cooking only one minute, or like thick cream by cooking it two minutes.

"Sometimes you want it thicker than others," said her mother, "so I just put that in to explain. To-day make it like thin cream. Now, Mildred, you can put it all together while Jack brings in the cold boiled potatoes and Brownie cuts them up."

CREAMED POTATOES

Cut eight large boiled potatoes into bits the size of the end of your thumb. Put them in a saucepan and cover them with milk; stand them on the back of the stove where they will cook slowly; watch them so they will not burn. In another saucepan make white sauce as before. When the potatoes have drunk up all the milk and are rather dry, drop them in the sauce; do not stir them; sprinkle with pepper.

"Now for the muffins, for it is after five o'clock. Brownie, you find the muffin pans and make them very hot. Do you know how to grease them?"

"Yes, indeed!" said Brownie, proudly. "This is the way." She got a clean bit of paper, warmed the pans, and dropped a bit of butter in each, and then with the paper rubbed it all around.

MUFFINS

2 cups of flour.
1 cup of milk.

1 rounded tablespoonful of butter.

2 eggs, beaten separately.

1 teaspoonful of baking-powder.

½ teaspoonful of salt.

1 teaspoonful of sugar.

Beat the egg yolks first; then add the milk; melt the butter and put that in, then the flour, well mixed with the baking-powder, then the salt and sugar. Last, add the stiff whites of the eggs. Fill the pans half full.

"Some things, like cake, cannot bear to have the oven door opened while they are baking," said Mother Blair; "but salmon does not mind if you open quickly; so, Mildred, put these in as fast as you can; they will take about twenty minutes to bake. I do believe that is all we have to make except the tea, and that takes only a moment when everything else is ready. I will give you the receipt for it now, and after everybody is here and you have said 'How do you do?' to them, you can slip out and make this, and while it stands you can put the other things on the table. But perhaps you had better make some coffee too; the men may like it."

TEA

Fill the kettle with fresh, cold water and let it boil up hard. Scald out an earthen tea-kettle, and put in two rounded teaspoonfuls of tea for six people, or more, if you want it quite strong. Pour on six cups of boiling water and let the pot stand where it is warm for just two minutes. Scald out the pot you are going to send to the table, and strain the tea into that. Have a jug of hot water ready to send in with it.

COFFEE

1 rounded tablespoonful of ground coffee for each person; and

1 extra tablespoonful.

½ cup of cold water.

1 egg shell, washed and broken, with a little bit of the white.

Mix these in a bowl. Then put in a very clean pot and add

> 1 cup of boiling water for each person and
> 1 cup more.

Let it boil up hard just once; stir it, pour in 1 tablespoonful of cold water; let it stand three minutes, strain and put in a hot pot.

She looked Carefully in the Oven Through a Tiny Crack

Just before the door-bell rang, Mildred went to the refrigerator to look at her custards and found them nice and cold. Then she looked carefully in the oven through a tiny crack, and found the muffins were done and the salmon beautifully brown; so she took up the potatoes, and put them in the covered dish on the back of the stove where they would keep hot, and asked Brownie to lay the hot plates around the table, one for each person. Then she went into the parlor and said "How do you do?" to the guests, and after a moment slipped out again, and put everything on the sideboard, made the tea, filled the glasses, and put butter on the bread-and-butter plates. Then Brownie asked everybody to come to supper.

When they had all sat down, Mildred passed the dish of salmon, offering it on the left side, of course, just as Norah always did; then she put the dish down before her father and passed the potatoes and muffins in the same way, while Mother Blair poured the tea and handed it around without rising from her seat. And then everybody began to eat, and say, "Oh, how good this salmon is!" and "Did you ever taste such muffins?" and "Did you really, really make all these good things yourselves, children? We don't see how you ever did it!" And they ate at two helpings of everything, and Father Blair ate three. And when it was time to take the dishes off, there was not a speck of salmon left, nor a spoonful of potato, nor even a single muffin.

Jack served the custards

Then Brownie quietly took the crumbs off as she had seen Norah do, brushing them onto a plate with a folded napkin; and as she was doing this, Jack slipped out to the refrigerator and got the custards, all as cold as ice and brown on top, looking as pretty as could be in their cunning cups; each cup was set on a dessert plate and a spoon laid by its side, and the fresh cakes were passed with them.

Soon after supper the company went home, and then Mildred said: "I feel exactly like a toy balloon—so light inside! Wasn't that a good supper? And didn't they like the things we had! And isn't it fun to have company! When I am grown up and have a house of my own, I shall have company every day in the week."

"I shall make a point of coming every other day at least," said Father Blair. "I'm so proud of my family to-night! Those Wentworths may be staying at the very best hotel in town, but I know they don't have such suppers there."

"Don't you wish you could cook, Jack?" inquired his mother, with a twinkle in her eye. And then everybody laughed, and said: "Dear me, what good times we Blairs do have together!"

CHAPTER VI

MILDRED'S SCHOOL PARTY

One day early in June, Mildred ran up to her mother's room as soon as she came home from school. She tossed her hat on the bed, and dropped her books in an arm-chair. "Oh, Mother!" she exclaimed, out of breath, "do you suppose I could have twenty girls here some afternoon for a little bit of a party! I do so want to ask them right away, before exams begin. They are my twenty most particular friends, and some of them are going away just as school closes, so, you see, I have to hurry."

"Of course you may have them," said Mother Blair. "But only *twenty* particular friends, Mildred? What about the rest of the class?"

Mildred laughed. "Well, I mean these are the girls I happen to know best of all, and I want to have a kind of farewell before summer really comes. What sort of a party shall we have, Mother? I mean, what shall we have to eat?"

"I should think strawberry ice-cream would be just the thing, with some cake to go with it, and something cold to drink; is that about what you had thought of?"

"Just exactly, Mother. But do you think we can make enough ice-cream here at home for twenty people? Wouldn't it be better to buy it?"

"Oh, I am sure we can easily make it, and home-made ice-cream is so good—better, I think, than we could buy. We can borrow Miss Betty's freezer, which holds two quarts, and as ours holds three, that will be plenty. We count that a quart will serve about seven,—more cooking arithmetic, Mildred! If one quart will be enough for seven people, how many quarts will be needed for twenty?"

"The answer is that five quarts will be just about right," laughed Mildred. "Perhaps some of them will want two helpings. But, Mother, if we have the party on Saturday, Norah will be very busy, and who will make the cream?"

"We will all make it together, and Jack may pack the freezers and turn them for us. And Norah may make the cake for you on Friday, so that will be out of the way."

So, early on Saturday morning, Mildred and Brownie began to hull strawberries for the party and put them away in bowls on the ice. Then they made the table all ready on the porch, putting a pretty little cloth on it, and arranging plates and napkins; glasses, for what Brownie called the "nice-cold drinks," were set out too, and little dishes of the candy which Father Blair had brought home and called his contribution to the party; and in the middle of the table they put a bowl of lovely red roses.

After an early luncheon, everybody went at once to the kitchen. The berries were put on the large table, and the cream and milk brought from the refrigerator. The two freezers stood ready in the laundry with a big pail for the broken ice, a heavy bag, a wooden mallet, and a large bag of coarse salt.

"Come, Jack," his mother said, as he stood picking out the biggest berries from the bowl and eating them, "here's some more man's work for you! We want you to break the ice and pack these freezers for us."

"What do I get for it?" Jack asked, pretending to grumble. "If the girls are going to eat up all the ice-cream, I guess I won't bother freezing it."

"No, indeed, they are not going to eat it all up," said Mother Blair. "I am counting on having ever so much left over for dinner to-night; and you shall have two helpings."

"Make it three and I'll think about it," said Jack, choosing the very biggest berry of all.

"Three then," said Mildred, disgustedly, taking the bowl away. "Boys do eat so much!"

"This cream is going to be so good that you will want three yourself," laughed Mother Blair. "Now, Jack, this rule is for you. Some cooks think that all you have to do in packing a freezer is to put in layers of broken ice and salt, and then turn the handle; but there is a right way to do it, and if you follow this, you will find the cream will freeze ever so much more quickly than if you are careless in packing."

PACKING A FREEZER

2 large bowlfuls of broken ice.
1 bowlful of coarse salt.

Put the ice in a strong bag and pound with a mallet till it is evenly broken into bits the size of an egg. Put the ice in a pail till you have a quantity broken, and then measure; add the salt quickly to the ice and stir it well; then put the empty ice cream tin in the freezer with the cover on, and fasten on the top and handle. Pack the ice all around the tin tightly till it is even with the top. Then stand it away, covered with a piece of carpet or blanket, in a dark, cool place, for half an hour. There should be a thick coating of frost all over the inside when the cream is put in.

While Jack was working in the laundry, Mildred and Brownie were reading the receipt their mother gave them, and getting out the spoons and sugar and other things they would need.

"Are the berries washed?" asked Mother Blair. "Yes, I see they are; now, Brownie, you may put half of them at a time into this big bowl, and crush them with the wooden potato-masher till they are all juicy. And, Mildred, here is the rule for making one quart of plain white ice-cream; all you have to do is to add any kind of fruit or flavoring to this, and you can change it into whatever you want."

"Just like a fairy's receipt!" said Brownie.

"Exactly!" said their mother. "Now, Mildred, multiply this rule by five."

PLAIN ICE-CREAM

3 cups of milk.
1 cup of sugar.
1 cup of cream.
Flavoring.

Put the cream, milk and sugar in a saucepan on the fire, and stir till the sugar is melted and the milk steams, but does not boil. Take it off and beat with the egg beater till it is cold; add the flavoring and freeze.

FRUIT ICE-CREAM

1 quart of fruit, or enough to make a cupful of juice.

1 small cup of sugar.

Mash the fruit, rub it through a sieve, add the sugar, and stir into the cream just before putting it into the freezer.

"You see what an easy rule this is. You can use fresh raspberries or pineapple or peaches in summer-time, and in winter you can use canned fruit. If the fruit is sour, of course you must take a little more sugar than if it is very sweet. And when juice is very sour indeed, like currant or cherry juice, do not use it for ice-cream. And when you want to make chocolate ice-cream you put in—"

"Do let me write that down, Mother, please, because I perfectly love chocolate ice-cream," interrupted Mildred.

CHOCOLATE ICE-CREAM

Make the plain ice cream as before; while still on the stove add

3 squares of unsweetened chocolate, grated.

¼ cup of sugar.

2 teaspoonfuls of vanilla.

Put the vanilla in last, just before freezing.

It took only a little while to mix the cream and cool it, and then Brownie had the berries all ready to go in; so Mildred called to Jack to know if the two freezers were ready. Jack was reading "Treasure Island" in a corner of the laundry, and it took three calls to rouse him.

"The freezers?" he asked; "the freezers—oh, yes, they are all ready. At least I suppose they are, they've been standing so long. I've been having a great time with old *Silver* in the stockade!"

"Well," said Mildred, doubtfully, "if you've been off on one of your treasure trips, I don't know whether the freezers will be ready or not."

But when they looked inside, there was the thick frost all over the tin. "Perfect!" said Mother Blair. "Now you will see how quickly the cream will freeze. It makes all the difference in the world whether or not it is ice-cold inside." Then they poured in the cream and shut the freezer tightly, and Jack began to turn the handles, first of one and then of the other, with "Treasure Island" open before him on an upturned pail, though he very soon found that the freezers needed all his attention. He was devoting himself to his task with grim determination when Mildred peeped in at the door and stood watching him for a moment before she asked, mischievously, "And what is old *Silver* doing now, Jack? I believe you're really going to deserve those three plates of ice-cream, after all."

"Come, Mildred!" called her mother, "we will make something perfectly delicious to drink," and she handed a fresh receipt to the girls.

GRAPE-JUICE LEMONADE

4 lemons.

1 quart of water.

2 large cups of sugar.

1 quart of grape-juice.

1 orange.

Put the water and sugar on the fire and boil them two minutes. Roll the lemons and squeeze the juice; when the water is cool, add this and stand it away till you need it. Then add the grape-juice, and put it in a large bowl with a good-sized piece of ice; slice the orange very thin and cut into small pieces and add last. Serve in glass cups.

"That is so easy anybody could make it," said Brownie. "I guess I'll make some for us all on the next hot night."

"Oh, goody!" said Mildred. "Think how lovely it would taste out on the porch just before bedtime!"

"Specially if there was a moon," said Brownie.

"Yes, indeed! especially if there was a moon! You won't forget, will you?"

Brownie promised faithfully she would not.

By the time this was done and ready to put away in the refrigerator to get very cold, Jack was shouting for somebody to come and see if the cream was frozen. "It turns awfully hard," he complained, rubbing his arms.

His mother wiped off the edges of the tin very carefully so no salt could get in, and then lifted the cover, and, sure enough, the cream was firm and smooth, and a beautiful pink color. Mildred watched her carefully and took the second freezer, doing exactly what her mother did to the first one. They slowly pulled out the dashers, scraping them off as they did so, and then packed the cream down hard; the covers were put on again, each with a cork where the dasher-top had been. Meanwhile Jack had been told to break more ice and mix it exactly as he had before. When this was ready, the plug at the side of each freezer was pulled out and the water drained off, and then the cans of cream were buried in the fresh ice so that neither of them could be seen, a piece of carpet was laid over each, and it was put back in its dark corner.

"There!" said their mother, when it was all finished. "Ice-cream has to stand at least two hours after it is packed before it is quite good enough to eat. Thank you, Jack! You are really learning lots about cooking, aren't you? And now we will cut the cake and put it on plates in the refrigerator to keep fresh, and then we will all go and dress for the party, because it is three o'clock."

The Refreshments were Perfectly Delicious, Everybody Said

The refreshments were perfectly delicious, everybody said, and the girls said the pink ice-cream, and the sponge-cake, and the grape-juice lemonade were "the best ever." When everybody had gone, Mildred took a big plateful of ice-cream over to Miss Betty.

"Oh, how good that is!" she said as she ate it. "How *beautifully* good! So good to look at, I mean, as well as to taste. Would you like to have some more strawberry ice-cream receipts to go with it?" Mildred said she would love to, so Miss Betty began to write:

FROZEN STRAWBERRIES

1 quart of water.
2½ cups of sugar.
2 quarts of berries.
Juice of 1 lemon.

Crush the berries and press through a sieve; there should be two cups of juice; if not, add a few more berries. Boil the water and sugar one minute, cool, add the berry juice and that of the lemon, cool and freeze; serve in glass cups.

"You can see, Mildred," went on Miss Betty, as she finished this, "that a pretty way to serve this is to put each cup on a small plate and lay a few fresh strawberry leaves by it."

"Sweet!" said Mildred, and Miss Betty began the second receipt

ICE-CREAM AND STRAWBERRIES

1 quart of plain ice cream.
1 quart of large strawberries.
½ cup of powdered sugar.

Cut the berries in slices and lay them on a dish, and sprinkle the sugar over them. Take some tall glasses, put in a layer of ice cream, then a layer of berries; let the cream be on top, and put two or three whole berries on top of all. Or, if you can get little wild strawberries, use those whole both in the layers and on top.

"Those are both just perfect," sighed Mildred. "Now haven't you one more receipt, dear Miss Betty? Three is a lucky number, you know."

Miss Betty thought a moment "Well, here is something I think is just delicious, and it's so easy that Brownie could make it alone—or even Jack! There is no turning of the freezer at all, only the ice to be broken. But it must be made in good season, for it has to stand awhile, as you will see. And when you turn it out you can put a row of lovely big strawberries all around it and sprinkle them with sugar."

PARFAIT

1 cup of sugar.

1 pint of cream.

1 cup of water.

Whites of 3 eggs.

1 teaspoonful of vanilla.

Put the sugar and water on the stove and boil gently three minutes without stirring. Lift a little of the syrup on the spoon and see if a tiny thread drops from the edge; if it does, it is done; if not, cook a moment longer. Then let this stand on the edge of the stove while you beat the whites of the eggs very stiff and slowly pour the syrup into them, beating all the time. While you are doing this, have somebody else beat the cream stiff; when the eggs and syrup are beaten cold, fold the cream into them, add the flavoring, and put in a mold with a tight cover. Put this in a pail, cover deeply with ice and salt as before, and let it stand five hours.

"You see how easy that is," said Miss Betty. "That's all the receipts to-day. But, Mildred, if you and Jack, and Brownie will all come to luncheon next Saturday, I'll have something else made out of strawberries for you."

"Oh, Miss Betty!" cried Mildred, rapturously, "we'll come—indeed we will!"

"Very well; and tell Jack he can have three helpings of everything!"

CHAPTER VII

STRAWBERRY TIME

Early in the morning of the next Saturday came a note from Miss Betty, which said:

Dear Mildred and Dear Brownie:

Just to think that I forgot to tell you I wanted you both to help me cook the luncheon for our party! Do come over at about eleven, and bring your aprons. And please tell Jack that if he wants to come and help too, I'll find him something perfectly proper for a boy to do.

Y

OUR LOVING BETTY.

"Oh, goody!" exclaimed Brownie, as she read the note over Mildred's shoulder. "The very best fun of parties is getting ready for them, and I know Miss Betty will have something nice for us to do."

"What do you suppose Miss Betty wants *me* to do?" asked Jack, curiously. "I just believe it's a joke, and she really means to get me to make cake, or some other kind of girl's cooking. I don't believe I'll go till lunch-time."

"Oh, it's an invitation!" said Brownie, much shocked. "You *have* to go! And it's Miss Betty, too!"

Jack laughed. "Well, all right," he said. "Miss Betty is such fun that perhaps I won't mind."

"Take your clean apron, Jack," said Mildred, teasingly.

"Pshaw!" sniffed Jack, with a lordly air.

Miss Betty's house was just across the lawn; when they reached it, she met them at the door and told the girls to go right in and get their aprons on. "Now, Jack," she said, dimpling, "I'm afraid I've brought you over under false pretenses, for I really don't want you to cook at all. I only hope you won't be too disappointed!

But the weeding man who takes care of the garden has not come to-day, and I want some strawberries. Would you mind picking some for me?"

Jack's sober face lighted. "Why, I'd love to do it! That's what I call a man's work, Miss Betty. How many do you want?"

"Well, I want two kinds; first about a quart of ordinary ones, and the rest the very biggest in the garden; here are two baskets for them, and you may pick in one as you go along, and in the other lay the big berries on the freshest, prettiest strawberry leaves you can find. I want eight berries apiece for us—let me see—eight times four—" but Jack was off before she finished.

"Now, girls," Miss Betty said, as she tied on her own apron, "we will go right out to the kitchen and begin. But first, Brownie, can you lay the table for us?"

"Cer-tain-ly I can," said Brownie, proudly. "You can just tell me what you are going to have to eat, and show me where you keep things, and I can do it all alone."

So Miss Betty gave her a pretty square lunch-cloth to put cornerwise on the round table, and showed her where she kept the napkins and silver and china. "We are going to have creamed chicken, and iced cocoa, and salad, and strawberry shortcakes," she said.

"Hot plates for the chicken," murmured Brownie, counting out four, "and cold plates for salad; tall glasses for cocoa; hot or cold plates for shortcake, Miss Betty?"

"Just warm, I think. I'll help you carry all these out to the kitchen so they will be ready when we want them. And are you sure you do not want me to help you put on the silver?"

But Brownie shook her head, and went on talking to herself as she arranged the forks:

"Never use knives except to cut up meat with; so forks for creamed chicken, and forks for salad, both on the right, because everybody is right-handed; and the chicken fork farthest away, because that comes first, and the salad fork next the plate, because that comes after. Shall I put on a fork or a spoon for the shortcake?"

"We shall need both, but I think we will lay those right on the plates when we put them on the table. Here are the finger-bowls; we will put them on these small, pretty plates with a little doily under each bowl; and to-day we will stand them at the top of the place, not directly in front."

"Mother always puts the fruit plate and finger-bowl right down in the middle of the front," said Brownie, doubtfully; "not at the top."

"That is the way when you are going to eat an orange or peach on the plate; but you will see by and by why it is different to-day. Now I know Mildred wants me in the kitchen, so I'll leave you to finish the table all by yourself."

As soon as Miss Betty appeared, Mildred asked, "Now what first?" and pushed up her sleeves.

"First we must start the salad. I really ought to have done that long ago, but I waited for you. It is much better when it stands."

She brought in three large tomatoes and washed them and cut out the stems. Then she put them into a saucepan and poured boiling water over them, and, after they had watched a moment, they saw the skin all around the edge of the stem-hole begin to curl up; then they poured off the water, and Miss Betty put a fork into one and with a small sharp knife quickly pulled off all the skin; then she gave the fork to Mildred, and let her finish the others and put them away on the ice while she washed the lettuce and rolled it up in a towel and put that on ice, too, to make it get crisp. Then she read her this rule:

PLAIN TOMATO SALAD

Scald and peel the tomatoes, and put them on ice for an hour. Wash the lettuce after separating, roll in a towel, and put on ice also. When it is time to use the salad, slice the tomatoes and arrange with the lettuce on plates or in a bowl. Make the usual French dressing, and put it in a cream bottle; just before using, shake this very hard and pour over at once.

"You know how to make French dressing, don't you, Mildred?"

"Oh, yes, indeed! I learned that long ago, when I was putting up luncheons for Jack. But I never put it in a bottle—I just mixed it in a bowl."

"My dear, I've only just learned to put it in a bottle! You will be surprised to find how much better it is for a hard shaking, such as you cannot give it in a bowl. It is thick, and so well mixed that it is twice as good. I found that out myself the other day.

"And here is a special receipt for you, Brownie," continued Miss Betty, as Brownie came into the kitchen; "such a cunning little one!"

YELLOW TOMATO SALAD (BROWNIE'S)

Scald and peel little yellow tomatoes; chill, and lay on lettuce leaves; add French dressing just before serving, or mix the yellow tomatoes with little bits of red ones.

"Oh, that must be lovely!" said Brownie. "I'm going to copy that in my book, and put my name after it, as my very own salad!"

"Now what next?" asked Mildred, as she set away the French dressing in the cream bottle.

"Delicious little strawberry shortcakes; do you remember your rule for biscuits?"

"Indeed I do! I've made those so often I never even look in my cook-book."

"Well, then, you may make a panful of those; only remember to roll the dough out very thin—not thicker than half an inch; and do not let the biscuits touch each other in the pan. Now, Brownie, here is a platter of cold roast chicken, left from dinner last night, for you to pick off the bones and cut up in little, even pieces about the size of the end of your thumb. Use the white meat first, because that looks best creamed, and if there is not enough, then use some of the dark. Here is the rule:"

CREAMED CHICKEN

1 large cup of thick white sauce.
2 cups of cold chicken in small pieces.
½ teaspoonful of salt.
½ teaspoonful of chopped parsley.
1 shake of pepper.

Make the usual white sauce, but use two tablespoonfuls of flour to one of butter, so it will be thick (see your rule). When it is done, add the seasoning and then the chicken; keep very hot, but do not let it boil again.

"You can serve this on squares of buttered toast, or just as it is in little dishes, or on one round platter."

Mildred's biscuits were all ready to go into the oven by this time, and Miss Betty said they were lovely, but told her to put a bit of butter on top of each one, so they would be brown. "Now copy off your rule," she added.

STRAWBERRY SHORTCAKES

Make the usual rule for biscuits, but divide it, unless you wish a good many. Butter the top of each biscuit; when baked, gently separate them into two layers. Put a little butter on each half. Crush some ripe strawberries and sweeten them; arrange the lower halves of the biscuits on a dish, or put one on each plate; cover with the berries, put on the tops, sift sugar over them, and add two or three berries to each. Pass cream with them.

"If some day you want to make one large shortcake, Mildred, all you have to do is to make one very large biscuit, and split it open just as you have done these small ones."

"Shall we make the cocoa now?" Mildred asked, as she finished writing her receipt.

"Here Comes Jack with the Berries, just in Time!"

"My dear, that had to be very, very cold for luncheon, so Ellen made it right after breakfast, and put it on ice; but it doesn't matter, because you know how to make that. However, as we can't put any ice in it—that makes it horrid and watery—you may put a piece of ice in each of these tall glasses to chill them, and that will help make the cocoa cold; we will take it out at the last moment and put the cocoa in. Here comes Jack with the berries, just in time!"

Jack had two baskets of them, one of the biggest, loveliest ones, all laid on pretty strawberry leaves. Those Miss Betty washed and dried and put on the ice at once, with the leaves; the smaller ones she gave to Brownie to hull after washing. Then she read this receipt aloud:

STRAWBERRIES FOR A FIRST COURSE

Wash, dry, and chill the berries, but do not hull them. Put a little paper doily on a small, pretty plate and arrange the berries on the leaves around the edge in a circle, the points toward the center; in the middle put a little heap of sifted, powdered sugar. To eat them, take them by the hulls and dip in the sugar.

"There!" she said, as she and Mildred finished arranging them, "don't they look pretty? I think for breakfast or luncheon they are delicious this way. Now you see, Brownie, why the finger-bowls had to go at the top of the plate; these small plates go right before you on the table, and when Ellen takes them off, she can take off the others, too. Aren't the biscuits done yet, Mildred?"

Mildred ran to look—she had forgotten all about them, but luckily they were exactly right, a beautiful brown. So she took them out of the pan and carefully opened them at the side, using a knife at first, and then tearing them gently apart so they would not be heavy. When Brownie finished the berries, Mildred crushed them a little and sweetened them, but did not put them on the biscuits; Miss Betty said that must be done only just before serving, or the crust would be soaked with the juice. So she helped fill the glasses with water, and put on the bread and butter and cocoa, while Miss Betty and Brownie arranged the salad on plates and put the hot chicken in little dishes, each with a bit of parsley on top. Then they all sat down and ate up the luncheon, and nobody could say which was the best thing, the beautiful berries, or the lovely hot chicken, or the ice-cold cocoa, or the salad, or the shortcakes—it was all so good.

When they had finished, Mildred said there was only one fault to find with the lunch—that they had strawberries only twice.

"That's exactly the way I feel!" nodded Miss Betty. "In strawberry time, I want to have them in the place of meat and potatoes and bread, and everything else, and at least at all three meals a day, and between times, too! Now would you like some more strawberry receipts for your cook-book?"

"Yes, indeed!" said Mildred, running to get a pencil. Then Miss Betty gave her these:

STRAWBERRY CAKE

1 small cup of sugar.

½ cup of butter.

1 cup of cold water.

1 egg.

2 cups of flour.

3 rounded teaspoonfuls of baking-powder.

Put the baking-powder in the flour and mix well. Rub the butter and sugar to a cream. Beat the egg without separating, and add this; add a little water, then a little of the flour, and so on till all is in. Bake in two shallow tins. When done, and just before serving, put a layer of crushed, sweetened berries between the two layers and cover the top with whipped cream dotted with whole berries. Or cover with powdered sugar and whole berries and pass plain cream.

"This rule makes perfectly delicious raspberry or peach shortcake, too. Try it as soon as raspberries come, Mildred, for you will love it. Now just one more rule, and this is especially for Brownie."

STRAWBERRY RUSSE

Get a dozen ladyfingers, split them in halves, and cut each one in two. Arrange these around the edge of small glasses; fill the centers with berries cut in halves and sweetened, and cover with whipped cream; put one berry on top of each.

"Oh, Miss Betty give me one more, please!" begged Brownie. "I love special ones, just for me."

"Very well; here is one of the cunningest ones you ever saw."

BOX SHORTCAKES

Get from the baker's some small, oblong sponge-cakes; with a sharp knife mark all around the top edge, and then take out the middle part, leaving small, empty boxes. Fill these heaping full of sliced berries, or, if you can get them, small field berries, and cover the tops with powdered sugar; pass a pitcher of cream.

"Of course you can make little cakes at home for these instead of buying them at the baker's, but really, for this particular receipt, the bought ones are better. Hark! Isn't that your mother calling?"

It was, so they called Jack, who was reading "Kim" in the library, and all went home.

CHAPTER VIII

IN CAMP

"I've a nice long vacation ahead of me," announced Father Blair at breakfast one hot summer morning, "and I've set my heart on going to Maine on a camping trip. I don't want any guide to take care of me, yet I do need some one who will help me cook. I had thought of asking you to go, Jack, but as 'boys don't cook'—of course—"

"Oh, but they do camp cooking!" Jack exclaimed enthusiastically; "all sorts of things—bacon, and fried eggs, and corn-bread—"

"But, you see, you can't make any of those, and my digestion being delicate, I don't feel that I can be experimented upon," said his father, with a twinkle in his eye. "Now if only you had taken lessons all these months as the girls have, I might consider taking you."

"I'll learn right off, honestly I will! I'll begin this very day. And I can make cheese dreams, and—and boil eggs, now."

"How long do you boil them, Jack?"

"Till they're done!" said Jack, triumphantly.

Father Blair went off laughing, and said he was afraid he wouldn't be able to stand his son's cooking.

Jack spent a nervous day. Would his father really take him to Maine, to the camp in the woods he had always heard about, where his father and his men friends went nearly every year? Or would he be left at home merely because he did not know how to cook? At last he consulted his mother.

"I think Father will surely take you," she said comfortingly; "and he is just pretending about the cooking; he can do all kinds of camp cookery beautifully, and up there he will teach you himself how to make things."

So, sure enough, in just a week, Jack and his father were off for the woods of Maine, to a lake where the fishing was wonderful. They had a little log-cabin to sleep in, with a lean-to for their stores and cooking things, and there was a circle of stones, all blackened from other fires, where they could cook out of doors. The trees ran right down to the water's edge, and it was so still, and cool, and lovely that, if they had not been so hungry they could have sat and looked out at the lake for hours. As it was, as soon as they were settled and the guide had paddled off, they decided to have supper at once.

The first thing was to make a fire, and Jack brought an armful of twigs and began to lay them in the stone fireplace.

"No, that's not the way," said his father. "There are several kinds of camp-fires, and the one we want to-night is the quick one. You must get two green sticks, about three feet long, with crotches at the top, and stick them well into the ground so they will cross at the top; then you can fill the kettle with water and hang it up, two feet from the fire, and under it you arrange loosely some very dry small twigs; have some larger ones at hand to put on as they burn up; that makes a hot, quick fire; some campers call it a 'wigwam' fire, because they build it up in that pointed shape. To-night, however, the first thing to do is to start the coffee; this is the way to make it:"

CAMP COFFEE

1 pint of cold water.

3 heaping tablespoonfuls of ground coffee.

As soon as the water bubbles, and before it really boils, take the kettle off and let it stand for ten minutes where it is hot. Pour a tablespoonful of cold water down the spout to settle it.

While the coffee was making, they cut a large slice of ham from the whole one they had brought with them, and after the frying-pan was heated on the coals, they put this in it to cook. Then Jack got out four eggs to have them ready, while Father Blair gave him this simple rule:

HAM AND EGGS

Cut off the rind; when the pan is hot, put the meat in; turn often; season with pepper. Take up, put on a hot dish, and cover; break the eggs into the hot fat, and when they are set, turn each one carefully over and brown it.

The First Supper in Camp

"You cook bacon exactly in this way, too; only you must be careful not to cook it too long; you take it up when it is still transparent and before it turns to dry chips. Now, if you will get out the cups and sugar and condensed milk, and the bread and butter, supper will be ready."

They slept that night rolled up in their blankets in the bunks built on the cabin walls, and woke very early to hear the birds singing at the top of their little lungs. When they had had a dip in the lake and the fire was burning brightly and the kettle was on, Jack said he wanted more ham and eggs for breakfast.

"Not a bit of it!" said his father. "We are too far from civilization to have eggs every day; remember, the guide will not be back for a week with any more, and we must be saving of these. This morning we will have bacon—lots of it—and corn-cakes; by dinner-time, if we have any sort of luck, we shall have some fish to fry."

Jack Gets Breakfast

As they had two frying-pans, Jack used the smaller one on one side of the fire for the bacon, while his father, after mixing the cakes, baked them in the larger one. As the strips of bacon grew a little brown and curly, Jack took them up one by one and kept them hot till the cakes and coffee were ready too.

"Pour out all the bacon fat from the pan and save it," said his father, as Jack finished the last piece. "It's the best thing in the world to cook with in camp, for it flavors everything just as you want it. We'll need all we can get of it. And here's your receipt for the cakes."

CORN-CAKES

½ pint of corn-meal.
¼ pint of flour.
1 rounded teaspoonful of baking-powder.
1 rounded teaspoonful of sugar.
½ teaspoonful of salt.

Mix all together, and then gently add cold water and stir till you have a thick batter. Have ready a hot frying-pan, well greased, and put the batter in in spoonfuls; they will run together as they bake, but you can cut them apart; turn them over and brown on the under side.

After breakfast they heated some water and washed up all the dishes, made their beds, and picked everything up around the cabin. Jack hated to waste time doing this, he was in such a hurry to go fishing, but his father would not leave till it was all done. "Campers often let things go," he said, "and soon the whole place is full of empty tin cans, and half-burned sticks, and all sorts of rubbish, and it's a horrid place to live in. You'll find it pays to keep everything about a camp in decent shape. But now we will get off."

The lake was full of bass, and long before noon they had several fine ones, enough for two meals. "Some day soon we will go into the deep woods and fish for trout," said Father Blair. "This is too easy; trout-fishing is the real sport for us."

Then Jack had his first lesson in scaling and cleaning a fish, and found it no joke; however, after a time it went more easily, and then his father left him, to make a new kind of fire.

"This is what I call a lasting fire," he said. "The quick kind we made first goes out too soon to leave a bed of coals which we need to bake with. This is the way I do: I make a little pile of twigs just as before, but close up to a rock; then I stand several large sticks up in front and lean them back so they rest on the rock—so; then, as they burn, they fall down into the twig-fire and make coals. By adding wood from time to time I could keep this for hours. Now for my oven!"

He dug a hole about eight inches deep and a foot long right under the edge of the fire, and was soon able to fill it with hot coals. "When that is hot, say in ten minutes, I shall take the coals out and put my potatoes in."

BAKED POTATOES

Wash potatoes of even size; put them in the oven under the fire, cover with ashes, and put coals on top; new potatoes will cook in half an hour, old ones in forty minutes.

"Now how is your fish getting on? Luckily you don't have to scale all our fish; some you can skin, and some, like trout, you simply clean and cook just as they are. This is the way you do a good-sized fish:"

BROILED FISH

Scale or skin, clean, and wipe dry. Spread open the broiler and rub the wires with bacon rind or pork; cut the head off and split the fish open down the back, and lay it in; hold the broiler over the coals and turn it often; sprinkle with salt and pepper.

It was only a moment before the fish began to sizzle deliciously, and by the time it was done, the potatoes were done too, and white as snow after their black coats had been taken off. Together they made a wonderful meal, and there was enough fish left for supper.

WARMED-OVER FISH

1 pint of fish.

1 pint of hot mashed potato.

1 beaten egg.

Salt and pepper.

Use any kind of cooked fish, removing the skin and bones. Mix the ingredients, make into little cakes, and fry brown in a little hot fat.

BOILED POTATOES

Choose those which are the same size, so they will all be done at once. Peel them, dropping each one in cold water till all are done, and then put them in a pot of boiling, salted water, and cook gently half an hour. When soft, pour off the water, stand the pot, uncovered, close to the fire, and let them get dry. Eat them with salt and butter as they are, or mash them in the kettle, adding the same seasoning.

Jack cooked these, and mixed the cakes and got them all ready to brown. "What else are we going to have, Father Blair?" he asked anxiously. "I don't think these will be half enough."

"I think I feel just like pancakes," said his father, throwing down the book he had been reading. "I hope there's plenty of that prepared flour, Jack. I think I shall want about six cakes; how many will you need?"

Jack said he thought he could manage with eight, if they were pretty good-sized.

PANCAKES

Take two cups of prepared flour and mix with water (or use half water and half condensed milk) until it makes a batter like thick cream. Have ready a hot, greased frying-pan; pour in the batter from a small pitcher.

"Sometimes I have these instead of bread to eat with meat, and then we have gravy on them. Then sometimes we have maple-syrup, and call them dessert."

"Syrup for me!" said Jack, struggling to turn his fish-cakes without breaking them. "But I didn't know you were so much of a cook, Father."

"Jack, while we are eating, I'll tell you a true story, one of the dark secrets of my eventful life; that will explain to you why I believe a man should know how to cook."

So when the pancakes were finished and Jack had time to listen, his father told him the story of how, when they were first married, the Blairs had taken a trip across the prairie, and had camped a long way from a town; how Mother Blair had been taken ill and could not do the cooking, and poor Father Blair had to do everything for her and himself too, and did not know how to cook an egg, or make a cup of tea, or a bit of toast; and what a time it was! "I tell you, Jack, after that was over, I went to work and learned how to do a few things; and now, as you say," he added complacently, "I'm quite a cook. And the sooner you learn to cook, the better, for some day you'll need to know how; all men do."

"S'pose so," Jack murmured thoughtfully.

The Next Day was Perfect for Fishing

The next day was perfect for trout-fishing, so they started early with some lunch, and went back into the deep woods where there was a brown stream all full of little rocks and hollows, and there Jack took his first lesson in fly-fishing, and at night he was the proudest of boys when they looked at their basket of speckled beauties, four of which he had caught. It was great fun to cook them too, when they got back to camp.

SMALL FISH, BROILED

Clean the fish; put them on a green stick, passing it through their gills; put a slice of bacon or salt pork between each two fish; have a hot bed of coals, and hold them over this till done, turning often.

Several of the larger ones they strung on a string and put away in a dark, cool place among the rocks, and kept them till the next day, when they cooked them in a different way, and had:

PANNED FISH

Clean the fish; cut off the heads and break the spines, to keep them from curling as they cook. Put three slices of bacon or pork into a frying-pan, and, when this is done, take it out and put in the fish; cook quickly and turn often.

One day a rain-storm came on, so they could not go fishing, but had to stay in and play games and read and write letters. At noon, they went to a sheltered corner of the rocks and made a quick fire, where the rain could not reach it, and cooked their dinner; they had:

CORNED-BEEF HASH

1 can of corned beef.

1 onion.

2 large cups of cold boiled potato.

Pepper and dry mustard.

Cook the onion, after slicing it fine, in a little fat. Chop the potatoes and beef and add these, with the seasoning; when the under side is brown, turn it like an omelet.

For supper they had to go to their stores again; this time they had

STEAMED SALMON

Turn the salmon into a dish; take out the bones and fat, and pour away the juice; season with salt and pepper; put in a covered can and stand in a kettle of boiling water till very hot.

"We'll have fried potatoes with the salmon, Jack. Can you make those all alone?"

"Yes, indeed!" said Jack, who by this time could do a great many things.

FRIED POTATOES

Slice cooked or raw potatoes; heat a frying-pan, put in enough fat to cover the bottom when melted, and cook the potatoes till brown; scrape them up from the bottom often, so they will not burn.

The potatoes and salmon made a very good supper, but Jack was not sorry to hear that, when the guide made his weekly visit the next day, he would bring eggs and milk and vegetables.

"And I'm going to send for a little light sheet-iron stove made especially for campers," said Mr. Blair. "Then we'll have real corn-bread, and baked fish, and biscuits. Don't you want to learn to make biscuits like Mildred's, Jack?"

Jack grew red all through his tan as he looked at his father's teasing face.

"Well," he said doubtfully, "I suppose biscuits are all right, and I'll learn to make them if you say so. But, Father, you won't want me ever to make cake or desserts, will you? I draw the line there!"

"We'll see!" laughed his father. "Perhaps you'll change your mind about that, some day."

CHAPTER IX

IN CAMP (CONTINUED)

There was a wait of a week before the camp stove could arrive, and during that time, Jack took lessons in all sorts of cooking, and learned to make a number of good things; and this was fortunate, for one day two friends of his father surprised them; they were on their way to a camp farther in the woods, and wanted to stay a night and a day with the Blairs before going on. This meant that there were four people to cook for instead of two, and it needed all the experience Jack had to do his share of the work.

The visitors did not come until supper was done, and everything was eaten up; not even a bit of fish was left over. So the Blairs had to go to their stores and find something they could get ready quickly, and something very hearty as well.

"These fellows are as hungry as hunters," Mr. Blair said, while the men were washing up in the lake and getting ready for supper. "Here's some tinned meat; let's have that, with potatoes in it."

"But potatoes take so long to cook—"

"Not the way I'm going to cook them; only ten minutes. You can peel four and slice them very thin, and put them in cold water, and then peel and slice an onion while I open the meat and boil the kettle for coffee. Then I'll show you how to make a:"

TEN-MINUTE STEW

4 potatoes, sliced very thin.
1 onion, sliced thin.
1 can of tinned meat (not corned beef).
   Salt and pepper.

1 rounded tablespoonful of flour.

1 large cup of cold water.

Put the potatoes on to cook in a saucepan of boiling salted water. Then put the onion in a hot frying-pan with a tablespoonful of pork or bacon fat, and fry brown. Put the flour in the cold water and stir till it is smooth, and mix this with the onion and stir it up; when the potatoes are done, drain them and add next, and then put in the sliced meat and heat; do not boil.

By the time this was done, the coffee was ready too, and the nice hot stew was served with large cups of the coffee and plenty of bread and butter. With a second cup of coffee and crackers and cheese, their guests had made an excellent supper.

The next morning, Jack got up extra early, because he knew everybody would be anxious to go fishing. So he soon had the kettle boiling and the breakfast started, and cooked it all by himself while the men dressed. The principal dish was:

FRIED SALT PORK

Slice thin and put in a frying-pan with enough warm water to cover; stir it around till the water begins to simmer, and turn this all off and drain the pork. Then fry till crisp. Put this in a hot dish near the fire while you make the gravy.

1 tablespoonful of flour.

2 cups of boiling water.

A little pepper.

Put the flour in the grease in the frying-pan, and rub till smooth and brown; add the water slowly, stirring all the time, and then the pepper; when smooth and a little thick, pour over the fried pork.

With this he had pancakes, plenty of them, which were delicious with the pork gravy, and on these, with plenty of coffee, the men said they could get along very comfortably till dinner-time.

For dinner they had some of the fish they caught, broiled, with boiled potatoes; and, for dessert, corn-cakes and maple-syrup. For supper Jack took the fish left from dinner and made:

FISH-BALLS

1 pint of cooked fish, picked up small.
1 quart of hot mashed potato.
1 tablespoonful of butter.
A little pepper.

Beat all together till very light, and make into balls the size of an egg. Have ready a pail of very hot fat, and drop in two balls at a time and cook till light brown; take them out; keep hot; and put in two more, and so on.

After this, he had something which had taken a long time to make, but he did not mind it.

FRIED CORN-MEAL MUSH

1 rounded tablespoonful of salt.
1 quart of yellow corn-meal.
4 quarts of water.

Bring the water to a hard boil in a kettle over the fire; mix the meal with enough cold water to make a thick batter (this is to avoid lumps). Drop spoonfuls of the meal into the water gradually, so it does not stop boiling; when all is in, stir steadily for ten minutes. Then put a cover on the pot and hang it high over the fire so it will cook slowly for one hour; stir occasionally so it will not burn; then pack tightly in a pan and let it get perfectly cold and firm. (The best plan is to let it stand all night if you can.) When you wish to use it, slice it, and fry in very hot grease in the frying-pan till brown.

The next day the men left, after saying they had had a fine visit and had never had such good things to eat in camp. Then Jack and his father had a quiet time till the guide appeared once more, his boat full of stores and his pockets crammed with newspapers and letters; and in the end of his boat he had a small sheet-iron stove. That they quickly set up under the edge of the lean-to where, if it rained, it would not get wet and rusty.

"And now, Jack," said his father, rubbing his hands, "you shall taste my baked beans. I may say without boasting that they will be the very best you ever ate in your life. Women may be able to cook ordinary food, but it takes a man to cook beans—and I'm the man!"

Jack laughed, and said he wanted to learn how so he could beat his father making them, and he watched carefully everything that was done.

BAKED BEANS

Pick over a pint of beans and throw away all that are shriveled and poor. Wash the rest and put them in cold water to cover them, and let them stand all night. The next day, put the beans in fresh water and gently cook them half an hour, skimming them occasionally.

In another kettle, put a piece of salt pork as large as a man's fist; cover it with water and let it cook till the beans are done. Then drain the water off both, and cut the pork in two pieces; slice each piece part way down, leaving the lower portion solid. Put one piece in the bottom of an earthen dish, and pile the beans around and over it, and put the other piece on top. Mix

½ teaspoonful of salt.
¼ teaspoonful of pepper.
1 tablespoonful of molasses or sugar.
½ teaspoonful of dry mustard.

Pour this all over the beans and cover the pan; put in the oven, and bake at least two hours; uncover and brown during the last twenty minutes. If the beans get very dry, pour on half a cup of boiling water when they are half done.

"Aha!" said Father Blair, as he put the pan in the oven when they were ready to bake. "Those will be simply fine. Now we could have made them by putting them in a kettle over the fire and baking them so, or we could have buried the kettle in a hole in the ashes; but they are really better done in an oven if one happens to have one. And, anyway, I needed a stove to bake biscuit in, so that's why I got one. I think we will make some for supper, too, and put them in when the beans come out. The name of the one big biscuit I'm going to make to-night is:"

CAMPER'S BREAD

1½ pints of flour.
1½ rounded teaspoonfuls of baking-powder.
½ teaspoonful of salt.
2 rounded teaspoonfuls of any kind of fat (lard is best).
½ pint of cold water.

Put the baking-powder and salt in the flour; mix well and then rub in the lard till there are no lumps left and it does not stick to the pan; add the water, a little at a time, and stir with the spoon till smooth. Grease a pan and put the dough in in rather a thin layer; smooth the top and bake, till, when you put in a sliver of wood, it comes out clean. Eat while warm; do not cut, but break into pieces.

"Now I could have cooked this just as I could have cooked the beans, without the oven. I could have put it in the frying-pan in a bed of hot ashes and covered it and put ashes on top and let it cook till done; but it's better to cook it this way if you can, because it's lighter and browner. When you want regular biscuits, all you do is to make the dough into little balls, and be sure you put flour on your hands before you try it, Jack, or you'll get into an awful mess. And then you put them in the pan and just bake them till they are done."

"I like the big loaf," said Jack. "It's more like real camp cooking; biscuits are for a house."

"And now we are going to have something extra good to-day—green corn on the cob. I tell you that's a luxury for campers! How will you have it, boiled or roasted?"

"Both," said Jack, who liked corn immensely.

"Very well, but one way at a time, young man! We will have it boiled this noon, and we will roast it over the coals to-night."

BOILED CORN

Have a deep kettle full of water boiling hard; take off the husks
and silk, and boil the ears hard for twenty minutes; serve with
butter and salt.

"Some campers boil the corn in the husk and think it is better that way, but I find I always burn my fingers taking off the leaves and silk, so I believe in peeling it as we do at home," said Jack's father, as he put the ears in the kettle slowly, so as not to stop the boiling of the water. "Now for supper, this is the way to fix it:"

ROAST CORN

Take off the husks and silk. Put a stick in the end of the ear, and
toast it brown over a bed of coals; have ready butter and salt to
put on each.

Roasting Corn Over a Bed of Coals

The baked beans proved all their cook promised they should be, and almost the best thing about them was that they were just as good cold as hot, and so saved cooking things sometimes when they were in a hurry.

One day, they caught a perfectly huge fish, too large to broil well, and then their little stove proved a treasure, for the oven would just hold a baking pan; they cooked it in this way:

BAKED FISH

Clean and scale the fish, but do not take off the head or tail. Slice an onion fine, and fry brown in two tablespoonfuls of fat; add to this a cup of fine, dry bread crumbs and a little salt and pepper, and stir till brown. Wipe dry the inside of the fish, and put this stuffing in; wind a string around the outside to hold it firmly in place. Put in a pan with four slices of salt pork or bacon, and lay three or four more on the top of the fish; shake a little flour, salt, and pepper over all. Bake in a hot oven till the skin begins to break open a little; every fifteen minutes open the oven door and baste the fish; that is, pour a spoonful of juice from the pan over the fish; if there is not enough, pour a small cup of boiling water into the pan.

With this they had

BOILED ONIONS

Peel onions of about the same size, and drop them in a kettle of boiling, salted water; when they have cooked half an hour, throw this water away and put them in fresh boiling water. This will prevent their being too strong. Cook for one hour altogether. Put melted butter, pepper, and salt over them.

Before they could possibly think it was time to go home, their vacation was over.

For dinner, the last night, Father Blair made something very good indeed:

CAMP PUDDING

½ pound of dried prunes.
8 slices of bread, cut thin and buttered.
½ cup of sugar.
1 tablespoonful of butter.

Wash the prunes and cover them with cold water, and let them stand all night. In the morning, put them on the fire in this water, and cook slowly till they are very soft; then take out the stones. Line a dish with the bread, cut in pieces, with a layer on the bottom; put on a spoonful of prunes and juice, then a layer of bread, and so on till the dish is full, with bread on top; sprinkle with sugar and bits of butter and bake brown.

"My, but we've had a good time!" said Jack, thoughtfully rubbing the end of his sunburned nose as he watched the shores of the lake fade away the next day. "I never supposed it was such fun to camp. And I've become quite a cook; now haven't I, Father Blair?"

"I should say you had. Too bad your mother and the girls can't know about it. But they will never know!" and his father smiled mischievously.

"Well, perhaps some day I'll cook something for them," said Jack, sheepishly. "I don't mind knowing how to cook as much as I thought I should, now that I know men cook. I guess I'll surprise them some day, Father!"

CHAPTER X

JAMS AND JELLY

Norah was preserving peaches. The fragrant odor filled the house one day, and Mildred sniffed it delightedly. "Dear me! I wish I could make preserves," she sighed. "Norah's always look so lovely in their jars, and they taste so good, too. I wonder if she would let me help her?"

But no, Norah would not. Peaches, she explained, must be done up very carefully, and nobody could do them up unless they knew just how.

"'But Norah, if You can't begin till You know how, how does Anybody ever Learn?'"

"But, Norah, if you can't begin till you know how, how does anybody ever learn? And I want to do them so much! Just see how beautiful yours are," and Mildred looked longingly at the row of jars on the kitchen table full of yellow peaches in a syrup like golden sunshine. "Oh, Norah!" she murmured pathetically.

But Norah was firm. Miss Mildred couldn't do up peaches; she was too young; and, anyway, she couldn't be bothered teaching her. So Mildred sighed and gave it up. But when she told her mother about it, Mother Blair laughed.

"You want to begin at the top," she said, "Norah is quite right in saying that peaches are not easy to put up—that is, not the very best, most beautiful peaches, and nobody wants any other kind. But why not make something else to begin with, jams and jellies and other good things? And by the time you know all about those, you will find that peaches will be perfectly easy for you."

Mildred brightened up. "Now that's what I call a good idea, one of your very best, Mother Blair. Can't I make something right away to-day?"

"Just as soon as Norah is all through with her preserving, if she doesn't mind, you may. And perhaps she has something all ready for you to begin on. Run and ask her if you may have the parts of the peaches she did not want to use."

That puzzled Mildred, and as she hurried to the kitchen she thought about it.

"Norah, Mother says you are not going to use all the parts of the peaches, and perhaps I may have what you don't want. But what are they? Because if they are just the skins and stones, I don't want them either."

Norah was just fastening on the last top on her jars of preserves, and she looked very good-natured.

"Sure, I've got lots left!" she said, and showed Mildred a large covered bowl filled with bits of peach pulp.

"I won't put any bruised peaches in preserves," she explained, "so I just cut up peaches with soft spots and put 'em in here; and when I'm done, I make a shortcake out of 'em. If I've got enough, sometimes I make 'em into—"

"Jam!" interrupted Mildred. "Of course! delicious peach jam that I love. Oh, Norah, do let me make some; don't use any of those peach bits for shortcake —let's have something else for lunch."

"Well," said Norah, "I guess you can have 'em." So Mildred ran for her apron and a receipt, which, when she read it over, proved, strangely enough, to be a rule for making not only peach but all sorts of jams.

JAM

Prepare your fruit nicely; strawberries must be washed and hulled, peaches pared and cut up, raspberries looked over for poor ones. When they are ready, measure

> 1 large cup of fruit to
> 1 small cup of sugar.

Mash the fruit and put it in a kettle in layers with the sugar, and press and stir it till it is all wet and juicy. Then gently boil it, stirring constantly from the bottom up, so the fruit will not burn. Mash with a wooden potato masher till all is smooth. When it has cooked nearly an hour, try a little on a cold saucer and see if it gets firm. When it does, it is done. Some jams take longer to cook than others, because some fruits are more juicy.

This sounded very easy indeed, and Mildred began to mash and measure at once, and soon the jam was over the fire. But it took a long time to cook. Norah brought a dishpan full of jelly-glasses and put them in the sink, and Mildred washed these and dried them and arranged them on two trays, all ready for the jam; but every moment or two she stirred the jam well. By and by, after more than an hour, the peaches looked transparent, and then Norah said they were done; and, sure enough, when she hurriedly put some on a saucer and stood this on the ice in the refrigerator to get it cold quickly, it grew a little stiff and the edges were like jelly.

"I am so Proud, I want Everybody to see my Jam"

Mildred carefully lifted the hot saucepan from the fire and began to dip out the jam with a cup and put it in the glasses; when she finished, there were eight of them, all filled with clear golden-pinky-brownish jam, beautiful to look at, and, oh, so good to taste! Mildred ran for her mother and Brownie to look at it. "I wish Father and Jack were here," she sighed, "and Miss Betty, too. I am so proud, I want everybody to see it."

"It really is lovely," said her mother. "I never saw any that was nicer. Next winter we will eat it on hot buttered toast, and put it in layer cake, and have it ready for school sandwiches."

"But only eight little, little glasses," mourned Mildred. "Why didn't I make eight dozen of them?"

"Well, eight dozen is a good many," laughed her mother. "Perhaps—just *perhaps*, you know, you might find you got tired even of peach jam before you had eaten all those up. But the beauty of making jams in fruit time is that you can make a few glasses of it any time you want to. Peaches are just in season now, and we have them nearly every day, so you can put up more at any time."

"Of course!" said Mildred, delightedly. "I never thought of that. I'll make the rest of my eight dozen yet, Mother Blair; I'm sure it won't be a bit too much."

"Why not make some other things that are just as good? Grapes are in season too, and plums, and pears—"

"I'll make them all! I'll make every single kind of jam that there is!"

"You can make jelly too, and compotes, and spiced things; I'll be so glad to have you learn, and they are all as easy as can be."

"But, Mother, what can *I* make?" Brownie looked very sober. "Is Mildred going to make everything all alone? I like to make things, too."

"Of course you do, and you shall certainly help; jams are so easy anybody in the world can make them."

"Even Jack?" laughed Mildred.

"Yes, even Jack, if he wanted to. Why don't you and Brownie together make some nice grape jam to-morrow?"

The girls said they would love to; then their mother had them write down a special receipt, because grape jam is the one kind that is different from every other.

GRAPE JAM

Wash the grapes; take them off the stems one by one as though you meant to eat them, but press them between your fingers and put the skins in one dish and the pulp in another. When you have finished, heat the pulp and stir it till you can see that the seeds have come out; then put the pulp through the colander. Add this to the skins, measure, and follow your regular rule.

This seemed like a queer receipt; grape skins in jam! It sounded rather horrid. But they made it, anyway, and when they had finished, though it was a clear, reddish black, it was really delicious.

It happened that the grapes grew in their own garden, and so many of them were ripe that, when they had used up quite a large basketful, there were plenty left. Norah had been planning to use them in jelly, but she said she could wait a day longer for that, and the girls might have them if they wanted to, and she would show them how to make something very good indeed and very easy. This was:

SPICED FRUIT

3 pints of fruit, all prepared.
1½ small cups of vinegar.
1¾ pints of sugar.
2 teaspoonfuls of powdered cinnamon.
1 teaspoonful of powdered cloves.

Boil till thick; about an hour and a half.

In making spiced grapes, prepare them exactly as for jam, and use pulp and skins.

Their mother did not know they were making this new kind of preserve, and she was delighted when she was shown all the little glasses of it.

"All spiced fruits are especially nice with meat," she said, "and with this rule you can spice almost any kind of fruit; pears, or peaches, or apples, or plums—"

"Or strawberries, or pineapple, or raspberries," said Brownie.

"Oh, no! I ought to have said any kind of *autumn* fruit—that is a good way to remember which ones to use. And, Mildred, Norah divided this rule for you, to make it easier, but when I put up spiced fruit, I take twice as much of everything."

"What a pity I'm so stupid about arithmetic!" sighed Mildred. "Think of having to take twice one and three quarter pints of sugar, and twice one and a half cups of vinegar! I'll never get them right."

"Mildred, you remind me of a story some one told me the other day, about a girl who had just come home from college; it's a true story too, and the girl lives right in this town. She thought she would like to learn to cook, so she found a rule for cake in the cook-book and read it to herself; it began something like this: Three cups of flour, two cups of sugar, three teaspoonfuls of baking-powder, and so on. Presently her mother went into the kitchen and found on the table three cups, all filled with flour, two more cups filled with sugar, one cup of milk, another cup of raisins, three teaspoons in a row, all filled with baking-powder, and so on. Think of that!"

"I s'pose they didn't teach multiplying in that college," said Brownie, sympathetically.

Mildred and her mother laughed. "Well, I suppose I'll just have to learn to do fractions in my head!" said Mildred.

"There isn't any other way, if you are going to be a good cook," her mother replied. "You can't guess at things, or you will spoil them; you have to measure exactly. Now that you have finished these grapes, I'll give you some more receipts, if you want them."

The girls hastened to bring out their pretty red-covered books. "Just see, Mother Blair," said Mildred, turning over the leaves, "how many pages are filled up—with *such* good things, too!" And she gave a sigh of such complete satisfaction, that her mother laughed. Then they settled themselves at the table to write the new receipts.

APPLE CONSERVE

4 pints of apples, measured after they are peeled and cut up in bits.
4 pints of sugar.
2 lemons, juice and grated peel.
2 large pieces of preserved ginger (the kind that comes in little pots).

Mix all together and cook till thick; about an hour and a half.

CRANBERRY CONSERVE

2½ pints of washed and chopped cranberries.
2½ pints of sugar.
2 large oranges.
1 pint (or package) seeded raisins, chopped a little, after washing.

Cut the oranges in halves and take out the pulp with a spoon; then scrape the skins well till they are clean and not very much of the white lining is left; chop the rest. Mix all together and cook till thick.

"These two conserves are so very nice that we do not put them on the table and eat them up any day in the week, but save them for Sunday night supper and other times like that," said Mother Blair; "and sometimes they can go into sandwiches for afternoon tea. Now would you like just a very easy jelly? Here is a nice one."

APPLE JELLY

Wash twenty red apples that are not very sweet; cut them up in small pieces without peeling them or taking out the cores. Put them in a kettle and just cover them with water; cook slowly till it is all like soft apple-sauce. Then put it in a bag—a flour sack is the best—tie up the top, and hang the bag up over night with a large bowl underneath to catch the juice. In the morning measure this. Mix

1 pint of juice.

1 small pint of sugar.

Put on the fire and boil gently twenty minutes, skimming it occasionally; lift off the saucepan and drop into the jelly one large lemon, cut up in quarters, squeezing them a little; then put a small wire strainer over each jelly-glass in turn and pour the jelly into each from a cup.

"There! When you can make that kind of jelly, you will almost have learned how to make any other kind. And this is lovely, so pink and delicate, and it always gets just firm enough and not too stiff to be nice. Now, Mildred, you may try this to-morrow if you like, and, if it's perfect, you shall have a prize."

The next day the jam was firm on top, and Norah said it ought to be covered and put away at once or it would get too hard.

"How shall I cover it, Mother?" Mildred asked anxiously. "Paste on papers or something?"

"Oh, no, indeed! nobody does that way any more. Ask Norah if she has any paraffin left over."

But no, she had used every bit she had to cover her grape jelly; so Brownie had to go to the drug-store and get ten cents' worth. It came in a large cake, so clear and white it looked good enough to eat, but it wasn't, as the little girl found out by tasting. It was just like candles, and only mice like to eat candles. Norah said she would show the girls how to cover jams and jellies and spiced things, and everything you put in jelly-glasses.

"You take this little saucepan that I keep on purpose for paraffin," she said, "and put the whole cake in it after you cut it in two, and melt it; only be careful and don't let it splash on my clean stove and make it greasy. And while it is melting you can wipe off the jam glasses with a warm, wet dish-cloth and make them all clean and dry."

While Brownie was washing off the glasses Mildred cut some little slips of paper and printed on these the names for the different things they had made; PEACH on some, and SPICED GRAPES on others, and GRAPE JAM or APPLE JELLY on the rest. Then she got the pot of paste from the library; by this time the paraffin was melted and all ready to use. Norah showed them how to pour a little on top of each glass, right on the jam, and then tip the glasses a little so it would run up the sides toward the top. In a moment it hardened, and was ready for the tin covers to go on so the mice could not get at it, and then they pasted the labels on, and it was done.

Norah helped carry the trays to the preserve closet and put them away in rows, being very careful not to tip them and slide the paraffin up the sides of the glasses. Then they stood and looked at them, and, oh, how proud the girls felt!

"I'll make some more to-morrow," said Mildred, "and some more after that, and some more after that, and some more after *that*!"

CHAPTER XI

A HALLOWE'EN SUPPER

"Hallowe'en next week. Wish we could do something nice," Jack said to Mildred as they put away their books one night at bedtime.

"So do I. I'm tired of school already, and here it is only October! Of course, I don't mean that I'm dreadfully tired of it, you know, only just a little bit tired. I think, if we could have something very nice indeed to do, I could get on till the Christmas vacation—or at least till Thanksgiving without making any great fuss."

Jack laughed. He knew that Mildred, like himself, was always ready to have a good time.

"Let's have a Hallowe'en party," he suggested. "Not a sheet and pillow-case party, either; we've had those till I can't even think of one without wanting to scream."

"And not one where you bob for apples and walk around the house backward. I've done both those till I never want to do them again. I mean some new kind of a party."

But they could not think of anything new that seemed exactly what they wanted; so the next day they went in to see Miss Betty after school and asked her about it.

"Why, a chafing-dish party, of course," she said. "That's exactly the thing to have. You make a lot of indigestible things to eat and then you go to sleep and dream of ghosts and goblins, and hear shivery noises and groans and such things—just what you want, on Hallowe'en! I can think of a lot of awfully good things to have, things warranted to give you nightmares."

Jack said that suited him exactly, but Mildred was not so sure.

"Don't you think we might have two or three different kinds of things," she suggested doubtfully. "Some of them, for the boys, might be pretty bad; and some others for the girls a lot better. *I* don't want to dream of ghosts!"

Miss Betty was willing to do this, but Jack objected. "Be a sport, Mildred!" he said. "Remember it's Hallowe'en."

"Well, we'll see," she said at last. "Perhaps I'll eat a few dreadful things just to see what will happen. Now what can we have? I can't use a chafing dish at all."

"Jack can," Miss Betty said, laughing. Jack's cooking never ceased to be a joke.

"I? I never cooked in one in my life, except cheese dreams, at the Dwights'," Jack assured her.

"A chafing dish and a frying-pan are just the same sort of thing, and you know you learned all about frying-pans in the summer, so now, of course, you must show what you can do. I'll give you the receipts and tell you just how to make the things, but you must use a chafing-dish; if you won't— then, of course, I won't be able to help with the party at all."

So Jack reluctantly promised to do his part. "Probably I'll spoil things and make a mess," he grumbled.

But Miss Betty refused to let him off. "Of course you can cook in a chafing dish," she assured him. "All men can, especially those who can do camp cooking, and you know you're an expert there, Jack! Now let's see what we can have."

"Do let's have oysters for one thing; they are just in season now," begged Mildred.

"Of course—they are just the thing; suppose we have pigs in blankets, and Jack shall make them, for they are easy and oh, so good! And, Mildred, you shall have a chafing dish, too, and make something else; and we can make things to go with them, so there will be plenty of supper for everybody. How many are you going to have?"

"Oh, we haven't thought about it yet, and we must talk it over with Mother and see what she thinks; but I know she will love the party, because she always does."

And so, sure enough, their mother did love the plan. A chafing-dish supper was *such* a bright idea, she said, and so like Miss Betty.

They decided to ask only eight guests, four boys and four girls. In case the food did not turn out to be what they hoped, it was better not to have too many to eat it, Jack thought.

Hallowe'en obligingly came on a Saturday, just as though it knew how convenient that day would be for everybody. Mildred and Brownie and Miss Betty and Mother Blair and Norah all helped in getting things ready, laying the table, filling the alcohol lamps of the two chafing-dishes,—one borrowed from Miss Betty,—and preparing the good things for the supper. They decided to have first, the dish of oysters made by Jack at one end of the table, and some eggs to go with them, made by Mildred at the other. With these were to be some potatoes—a new kind Mildred had never heard of—and Brownie thought she could make these and send them in nice and hot; she was going to make cocoa, too, to go with the other hot dishes, and she and Mildred together were going to make sandwiches in the afternoon. And after these, Miss Betty said, there was to be something perfectly wonderful—something so good and so new.

"Oh, what?" they all begged.

Miss Betty's eyes rolled up to the ceiling, and she shook her pretty head. "Wait and see," she said solemnly. "I'll bring in the things this afternoon and we will all make it together." And they had to be content with this promise.

The table was laid just as they had it at breakfast and luncheon and Sunday night supper, with pretty doilies, one for each person and several over for chafing-dishes and piles of plates and sandwiches. In the middle was a big bowl of bright colored autumn leaves mixed with chrysanthemums; and at each place was a dainty card with a picture of a witch riding a broomstick, and the name of the boy or girl who was to sit there. The table looked very pretty when it was all finished, with the glasses and silver and small napkins. Brownie did it almost all alone; she loved to get ready for company.

Then they got out their receipt books and began to put down the different things they were to make for supper. Even Jack, smiling sheepishly, consented to write down the chafing-dish rules. They might come in handy when he went to college, he said.

PIGS IN BLANKETS

20 very large oysters.
20 slices of thin bacon.
A shake or two of pepper.

Wrap each oyster in one slice of bacon after you have cut off the rind, and pin it with a tiny wooden toothpick. Heat the chafing dish very hot by putting the upper pan, the one with the handle, directly over the flame. Lay in four or five oysters and cook them till the bacon crisps and the edges of the oysters curl; then take them up and put into a hot covered dish while you cook more. Have ready some strips of toast and put the oysters on two or three of these on hot plates. Shake a little pepper over them, but no salt, as the bacon will salt them enough. If too much juice comes out in cooking, pour it off and so keep the pan dry.

The oysters were all made up into "pigs" in the afternoon, and put in the refrigerator; they looked so funny when they were done—just like tiny pigs, all asleep. But as Jack thought twenty oysters for ten people were not enough, they made fifty. Then Mildred was given her rule:

SPANISH EGGS

Mix in the chafing dish.

1 tablespoonful of butter.
½ cup of gravy or strong soup.
1 onion, chopped fine.

½ cupful of thick tomato (canned).

1 green pepper, without the seeds, chopped fine.

Cook this fifteen minutes, stirring so it will not burn; then put into it:

6 eggs, beaten a little without separating.

1 teaspoonful of salt.

If, in cooking the vegetables, they get dry, put in a little more butter and tomato.

Miss Betty said if Mildred would stir this often she did not need to use the hot-water pan of the chafing-dish. "It takes so much longer to cook with it that I never use it if I can help it," she explained. "And now for the potatoes, Brownie."

SCALLOPED POTATOES

Wash and peel six large potatoes, and slice them thin. Butter a baking dish and put in a layer; sprinkle with salt and just a little pepper and dot with very little bits of butter. When the dish is full pour over it a cupful of milk and sift fine crumbs over the top, and add some more bits of butter. Bake for three quarters of an hour.

Like the oysters this dish was made ready in the afternoon, all but putting on the milk and crumbs.

"You don't need a receipt for cocoa, do you?" Miss Betty stopped to ask.

"No, indeed; we can make that with our eyes shut," laughed Mildred.

"Then we will go on to the sandwiches. Here are two kinds which are very good with oysters, and perhaps they may possibly give you ghost-dreams; I hope they will!"

TOMATO AND CHEESE SANDWICHES

Scald and peel some tomatoes and put them on ice till firm; then slice very thin indeed, and take out all the soft part and seeds; sprinkle with a little salt. Slice some white bread thin and butter it; lay a slice of tomato on a slice of bread and on top put a very thin slice of cheese—just a scraping of it; add the other slice of bread, press together and cut into attractive shape.

"I just happened to see the remains of that cold boiled ham you evidently had left over from yesterday, sitting in the refrigerator and looking lonely, so I planned these, which are much better than the common kind:"

DEVILED HAM SANDWICHES

Put some cold cooked ham through the meat chopper till smooth; add a very little dry mustard, a tiny pinch of black pepper and a very tiny one of red pepper. To a small cupful of the meat add two tablespoonfuls of melted butter and press into a cup; when cold spread this on buttered bread.

"My, those sound good," murmured Jack to himself, "and they sound like Hallowe'en, too."

"So they do," laughed Mother Blair, beginning to slice the bread and spread it. "Let's make them now and put them on ice, all rolled up in a wet napkin."

She and Brownie went to work, but Mildred said she was not quite ready yet. "I want another chafing-dish rule," she said. "Two are not enough, and they are all we have for our books."

"Well, just one or two more, and then I must fly," said Miss Betty; "you see I have to get the things for my own special receipt for the party. Here is a good one:"

PANNED OYSTERS, CREAMED

Take four oysters for each person. Make some slices of toast, butter them and cut them into rounds just the size to fit into the bottom of little brown baking dishes, or any small individual dishes which can go to the table. Put the oysters on these with a shake of salt and pepper for each and a bit of butter the size of the tip of your little finger. Put the dishes into the oven for ten minutes, or till the oysters curl at the edges; then take them out and put two teaspoonfuls of hot, thick, sweet cream on each, and a bit of parsley; stand each dish on a plate and send to the table.

"I know you will like that; now here is another:"

CREAMED EGGS

Take one egg for each person; put the lower pan over the flame and fill with hot water from the tea-kettle; put in the eggs and boil for ten minutes with the cover of the pan on. Take them out, peel them and wrap them in a napkin to keep them hot. Set away the lower pan, and in the upper one put:

1 tablespoonful of butter; melt this and add
1 tablespoonful of flour and rub together until smooth. Add
½ pint of cream or very rich milk, and stir till thick; add
½ teaspoonful of salt.
1 pinch of cayenne.
½ teaspoonful paprika.

Drop the eggs in and turn them over once or twice till they are very hot; serve each one on a round of buttered toast on a hot plate.

"Now that is positively all I can stop to give you now; I must begin on my own dish," said Miss Betty, putting on her hat. "But I'll be back again in just two minutes."

When she came she was carrying a huge pineapple, the largest the children had ever seen, and in a bag three large oranges and three bananas. "Now," she exclaimed as she put them on the kitchen table, "you shall see me make something very nice." This was the way she made it:

STUFFED PINEAPPLE

Get a large pineapple and cut off the brush at the top, but leave a little slice of the fruit on it, so it will stand. Scoop out the inside of the pineapple (and when you find a bit of the hard core do not put it with the rest but throw it away); cut the pieces all up into small dice. Cut the oranges in halves and take out the pulp with a spoon and mix with the pineapple; cut up the bananas and add these too. Then sweeten with powdered sugar. Set this away in a cold place. In serving it, fill the pineapple and put the brush on again and stand the fruit on a round dish with some heavy, stiff green leaves around it. The one who is served first is passed the plate; she takes off the brush and lays it by the side of the pineapple, and with a ladle dips out some of the inside on her dessert plate.

It took quite a time to prepare this, but they all liked to do it, and enjoyed the surprise it was going to be when it was first passed. Mother Blair said she did *so* hope she might take off the pineapple's cover, and when they came to think of it, as she was always served first, of course she would!

Well, the Hallowe'en supper was a perfect success. Jack, though nervous, proved that his camping lessons were not wasted, and Mildred's chafing-dish was as easy to manage as could be. But the next day when they all talked it over, not one of the family and not one of the guests had had a single ghost-dream after all!

CHAPTER XII

WHEN MOTHER BLAIR WAS SICK

One day Mother Blair woke up with a very sore throat, and the doctor said, when he had looked at it, that she must stay in bed for a day or two, and that Brownie had better go visiting.

"But where can I go, school and all?" the little girl asked Mildred very soberly after the doctor had gone. "If I lose my goggerfy lessons now I won't be the top of the class, and I thought I was sure to be; and when I'm the very top of all, you know Father gives me a dollar."

"Perhaps Miss Betty would like to have you visit her," Mildred said; "wouldn't that be fun? You could come in every single day and see how things are going with us, and we could wave at you out of the window—Mother could, I mean,—and it would be just lovely. I'll run over and ask her if you may come."

Miss Betty said she would be perfectly delighted to have a visit from Brownie, and Mother Blair said in a very croaky voice that it was a bright idea. So that very morning Brownie packed a bag and Jack carried it over for her, and she went visiting.

Mildred found she could be excused from school for a day or two, so she became nurse; and Norah said she guessed she could run the house alone after all the years she'd been learning how; so everything was just as smooth as could be.

When her mother's room was made all tidy and she had settled down to take a nap, Mildred ran across to Miss Betty's house to ask her what to give her mother to eat.

"The doctor said soft things, because her poor throat is so sore. What do you think I'd better give her for lunch, Miss Betty?"

"Invalids have to have nourishing things, Mildred, strong soups and eggs and cereals with cream, and custards. Suppose you plan to have a cream soup for to-day and start a meat soup for to-morrow; it takes two days to make that kind, you know. And—let me see—with cream soup you might have an egg, I think, and perhaps junket; that is the very softest thing in the world. Then by night perhaps she can have cream toast; that is perfectly delicious; if my throat feels sore toward night, Mildred, will you please make enough for two? I just love it."

Mildred laughed and promised that she would.

"And soft boiled custard in a pretty glass cup; and tea, I suppose. By to-morrow she will be so much better that I think she can have ever so many other things. Shall I write out the receipts for you now? Here is a good one for the soup."

CREAM SOUP

(This makes one cupful.)

2/3 cup milk.
½ tablespoonful butter.
½ tablespoonful flour.
¼ teaspoonful salt.
1 shake pepper.
1 tiny slice of onion.
¼ cup of any hot cooked vegetable; measure after thoroughly mashing it

Scald the milk with the onion in it; then take out the onion and slowly mix the milk and vegetable. Melt the butter, rub the flour into it and stir till it is smooth; then pour gradually on the hot milk; add the seasoning, bring it to the point where it almost boils, strain it and put it into a hot cup.

"This is one of the rules you have to learn by heart, Mildred. It is very easy, you see, almost like a very thin white sauce with vegetable in it. You can use mashed potato, or peas, or corn or celery or carrots, or whatever you happen to have in the house to make it with, and if you multiply it four times you will have enough for a dinner soup."

"Multiply two-thirds by four—" Mildred began.

"Never mind now, my dear! It makes my head go round to hear you. Copy this instead:"

CHICKEN BROTH

3½ pounds of chicken.
3 pints cold water.
2 tablespoonfuls rice.
1½ teaspoonfuls salt.
1 shake of pepper.

Have the chicken cleaned and cut up at the market. Take off the skin and fat and wipe each piece with a wet cloth. Put it into a kettle with the cold water and let it slowly get hot until it almost boils. (You can tell by looking at the edge of the kettle; when tiny bubbles begin to form it is nearly boiling.) Then skim it carefully; let it cook slowly till the meat is very tender; try it with a fork. Add the salt and pepper when it is about half done. Strain it, and set it away to grow perfectly cold; then there will be a layer of fat on top; take this off, add the rice and put it back on the stove and gently cook it till the rice is done. Or, if you have any cooked rice, add a tablespoonful to the soup while it is very hot. Serve in a heated cup.

"Then Mildred, you see you will have all the chicken meat left; you can take out a bit of the best white meat and put it away for creamed chicken for your mother's lunch the next day, and have the rest on toast for the family dinner. Norah can make a little cream gravy to take the place of the broth you have poured off, and it will be ever so nice."

"So it will; Father just loves that kind of chicken. Now the junket, Miss Betty."

JUNKET CUSTARD

¾ cup milk.

1 tablespoonful sugar.

¼ junket tablet (buy at the grocery in a little package).

1 teaspoonful cold water.

¼ teaspoonful vanilla.

Small pinch of salt.

Heat the milk till it is just as warm as the tip of your finger; add the sugar, salt and vanilla. Stir the junket tablet in the cold water till it melts, and add this. Pour it all very quickly into small molds or glasses and set in a cold place at once. When ready to serve, turn out of the mold, or serve in the glass with a little sugar and cream. If you wish to make this in a hurry, use half a tablet of the junket instead of a quarter.

"You can change the flavoring of this, Mildred, when you get tired of vanilla. Try almond sometimes; or, melt half a chocolate square and mix with the hot milk; or put in the vanilla and serve scraped maple sugar with it, with thick cream; they are all good. Now for the egg; can you poach that, do you think?"

"I suppose I can, really, Miss Betty, because I've seen Norah poach eggs about a hundred times; but I think I'd like a rule for my book."

"Good idea. Here is one, then:"

POACHED EGGS

Put the frying pan on the fire half full of hot water; add half a teaspoonful of salt. Butter the inside of a tin muffin ring and put this in the pan. Break a fresh egg carefully into a saucer and slip it into the ring; the water should cover the egg. Put a cover on the pan and set it on the back of the stove and let it stand till the white of the egg is like firm jelly.

While it is cooking make a slice of nice toast; cut it into a circle, butter it and lay it on a hot plate. When the egg is done take a cake turner, butter its edge and slip it under the muffin ring and egg together and hold it over the pan till the water drips away; then take off the ring, slip the egg carefully on the round of toast, add just a sprinkle of salt and one of pepper, and a bit of parsley. Cover the plate till you serve it, to keep it hot.

"Now, Mildred, I think you had better run home and get out the things for your tray, and I'll come over just before lunch and help you lay it prettily, if you want me to. See if you can find a pretty, thin cup for the soup, and a plate that looks well with it, and something perfectly *dear* for the junket. And a little napkin, not a large one. I'll bring a flower; you know you always have to have a flower for a sick-tray."

"You do?" Mildred's eyes were round. "What for, Miss Betty? You don't eat a flower!" she giggled.

"No, but you can't eat so well without it, if you are sick. Just wait till you are, and you'll see."

So Mildred went home and got out all the things she could think of for her mother's lunch and laid them on one end of the kitchen table. Then she tiptoed into the sick room, gave her mother her medicine and a cool drink of water, and turned her pillow over. After that she went out to begin the lunch.

She found Norah had plenty of junket tablets, so first of all she followed the rule for that. It was very easy indeed, and in just a moment she poured half the junket into a little glass for her mother, and the other half into an egg cup-mold for Jack's lunch. She put both of these right on ice so they would be firm, and used half the tablet instead of a quarter as her rule suggested, to be perfectly certain the junket would be firm enough by noon.

"You must be sure not to let them stand one minute, Miss Mildred," said Norah as she watched her. "If you do, they'll never set at all."

"Why not, Norah? Couldn't I just set the dish on the table for two minutes before I put it away?"

Norah assured her that it was quite impossible. "Junket isn't like gelatine; it won't wait," she said. So Mildred hurried just as fast as she could.

Next she made the soup; she found a cup of spinach in the refrigerator, and used that exactly as the receipt said, and the soup was a lovely pale green color. She put this where it would keep hot, and then boiled the water to poach the egg.

Before this bubbled Miss Betty came in with a pink geranium in her hand, and two green leaves. These she put in a very slender clear glass vase she found in the sitting-room, just large enough for them. Then she began to help Mildred with the tray.

"First you cover it with a clean napkin or tray cloth; that's a nice napkin, Norah, thank you. Then you put on a glass of cold water, only half full so it will not spill. Then the plate for the soup cup; and the soup spoon at the side, with the fork for the egg, and the little folded napkin and a cunning little salt and pepper. Next you get the egg and toast ready, put them on a hot plate—*hot*, Mildred, not just a little warm,—and cover it up with a hot cereal dish turned over it, unless you happen to have a covered china dish that comes on purpose. Stand this at the back of the tray. Get the little junket ready, too, and put the glass on a small plate; but you need not put this on the tray. Let your mother eat the hot things first, and take off the dishes and put the dessert on the tray all by itself. You can get it while she is eating, you know. Then, last of all, you put on the vase of flowers. There— doesn't that look sweet?"

Mildred said it certainly did; then she began to poach the egg, and Miss Betty went into Mother Blair's room and put an extra pillow behind her shoulders and a scarf over her and opened the blinds. She drew a little table close beside the bed and laid a fresh white cover over it, and when the door opened and Mildred came in carefully carrying the white tray with the good things to eat on it and the pretty geraniums, her mother was delighted.

"Oh, how good it looks," she exclaimed. "Mildred, did you really make that soup? And poach that beautiful egg? And actually make that junket? Well, I never did see anything so perfectly lovely. I'm proud to have such a daughter!" Then she ate everything, and declared her throat was almost well already.

In spite of that, however, the doctor made Mrs. Blair stay in bed several days, so that Mildred learned to make quite a number of new dishes for sick people. For one breakfast she gave her cereal with cream and bits of dates; for one luncheon she had the chicken broth, and for one supper cream toast and baked custard; she had goldenrod eggs, too, when her mother's throat was better, and baked apple. All of these things she wrote down in her book so she would not forget how to make any of them.

CEREAL WITH DATES

1 heaping tablespoonful oatmeal.
1 cup of water.
¼ teaspoonful of salt.

Mix, put in a double boiler and cook for one hour. Five minutes before taking this off the fire stir in

4 dates, washed and cut into small pieces.

Serve with cream.

CREAM TOAST

2 slices of nice brown, dry toast.
¾ cup of cream.
½ teaspoonful butter.
½ teaspoonful flour.
¼ teaspoonful salt.

Rub the melted butter and flour; heat the cream till it scalds, or almost boils; mix together and pour slowly over one slice of the toast in a deep dish; then put on the second slice and pour the rest of the cream over that. Serve very hot.

GOLDENROD EGGS

½ tablespoonful butter.

¾ tablespoonful flour.

¼ teaspoonful salt.

½ cup hot milk.

Rub the butter and flour, and add the milk and salt. Have ready

1 hard boiled egg. (Boil ten minutes.)

1 slice of toast.

Cut the egg in half, take off the white part and chop it; stir this into the white sauce. Cut the crust off the toast and pour over; then quickly rub the egg yolk through the sieve and sprinkle over all. Keep the sauce and toast hot in the oven until you put on the yolk; serve very hot in a covered dish.

BAKED APPLE

Peel and core a large sour apple. Put in a deep-earthen dish, fill the center with sugar, and just cover the bottom of the dish with water. Bake in a hot oven till soft, basting every five minutes with the syrup in the bottom of the dish. (That is, with a spoon pour the juice over the apple.) Serve hot or cold, with cream.

Mildred could already make baked custard, so she did not need a new rule for that. But soft-boiled custard she had to learn.

SOFT CUSTARD

1 cup of rich milk.

2 eggs.

1 tablespoonful sugar.

½ teaspoonful vanilla.

Put the milk on the fire to heat; beat the yolks of the eggs, add the sugar and beat again; stir this into the hot milk, add the salt and stir till the whole grows thick like cream. Then take it off at once; be careful not to let it boil at all or it will be spoiled. Let it get very cold; put it in a glass, beat half of the white of one egg and add this just before serving. Or, whip one spoonful of thick cream and put this on top of the custard.

After Mildred had learned to make all these good things, she used to search her cook book for receipts for other things, and as her mother got better she made something new every day. By the time Mother Blair was perfectly well and strong again, she felt she had grown to be a real sick-cook. And the best thing of all was that the doctor said the reason her mother got well so fast was that she had had such nourishing and delicious things to eat!

CHAPTER XIII

A DOLL-AND-LITTLE-GIRL PARTY

Mother Blair had an old school friend coming out to spend the day, and she had written that she must bring her little five year old daughter with her. This wasn't a bit convenient for the Blairs, because Miss Betty was to give a luncheon for the older people, and Mildred had planned to go to town for the day; and, of course, Jack couldn't be bothered to help take care of a child. That, surely, wasn't man's work, he declared.

So Brownie saw that she must entertain the small Helen all by herself, and she sat down to think what she should do for her.

"Five years old," she said to herself. "That means dolls, I guess. I'm pretty old for dolls, but of course I *could* get Araminta down from the attic, only she's packed up so nicely that I hate to disturb her. I wonder if five year olds play games? Mother Blair, do you think we could play in the attic with Helen's doll and Araminta, if I get her out, or what can we do?"

"Helen has had a bad cough, dear, and I'm afraid her mother would think that she must stay where there were no draughts. Why don't you have a little bit of a party for her? We could ask four other children about her age—"

"Oh, Mother, *I* know! I'll have a dolls' party, and cook cunning things in tiny little dishes just big enough for dolls to eat. That would be perfectly lovely, and I know Mildred would help me make some of them the day before."

"That would really be ever so much fun," Mother Blair said. "Run and ask Norah if she has any very little tins and molds that you can use, and I'll look up some receipts for you. Brownie, that dolls' party is what I call a really bright idea."

Norah was not at all busy just then so she got a kitchen chair and hunted on the top shelf in the tin closet and found several things for Brownie. One was a little tumbler of heavy glass, half the size of a small jelly glass; it had been used in traveling one summer when the Blairs were younger. Then there were six muffin tins fastened together like a pan which were never used because they made muffins so tiny that Jack said six were only a bite. And beside these she found a little tin cutter meant to cut vegetables into shapes for soup; this one was a tube with a star on the end, or rather the outline of one. Norah said that it would make lovely little cookies, each one the size of a five cent piece. Brownie was delighted with it.

"But, Norah, we won't want muffins," she said. "I remember when I was five, I couldn't have even one for breakfast—not till I was about seven, I guess it was. And Mother says Mrs. Lane is just as partickler as can be about Helen."

"I know something you can make in 'em," nodded Norah. "Not muffins. You just wait. You make it out of rice, and rice is awful good for children."

So Brownie ran into her mother's room to tell her what they had found and plan the meal with her.

"Suppose you have a really nice luncheon for both the dolls and the girls," she said. "You can have the low sewing table and set it with small plates and little napkins and have low chairs around it; the four children could sit on two sides of the table and Helen at one end and you at the other, and the company could all hold their children in their laps and you need not have any doll at all because you are hostess. How would that do?"

"Perfectly lovely, Mother. And now what shall we have to eat?"

"How would you like a hot first course—perhaps some kind of chicken and potatoes, with jelly and little cups of cocoa!"

"Oh, yes, Mother; and tiny sandwiches!"

"Yes, indeed; and then some dessert that children like; will that be enough, do you think?"

"Well, if they are not so very hungry, I think it will be."

Mother Blair laughed. "I think it is all their mothers would want them to eat for luncheon, anyway. Now what did Norah find for you?"

Brownie told about the little muffin tins, and said Norah said they could have something made of rice in them; and there was a little star cooky cutter and a little bit of a tumbler.

Mrs. Blair said they were all exactly what would be needed.

"I rather think Norah meant to use the muffin tins for these, Brownie. See how easy they are to make, and so good, too."

RICE PATTIES

1 heaping tablespoonful of rice.

2 cups of cold water.

½ teaspoonful salt.

1 teaspoonful butter.

½ an egg.

1 large cupful of cooked chicken, cut into bits.

1 small cup of thick white sauce. (See your rule.)

Wash the rice and put it over to cook in the double boiler in the water; add the salt; when it has cooked twenty minutes without stirring, taste it and see if it is soft, and notice if the water has boiled away so it is dry; if it is done, take off the cover and stand the boiler in the oven or on the back of the stove till each grain of rice is full and there is not a drop of water left. Then mix with the egg after you have beaten it and divided it, and put a spoonful into each muffin pan after it has been buttered; press this on the sides and bottom like a thick pie crust; warm the butter and put a little on the edges of each and put them in the oven till brown. Make the white sauce, heat the chicken in it and fill the patties at the last moment; put a bit of parsley on top of each one.

"We used to have these patties often for lunch and Norah would put in creamed fish or left-over vegetables, or eggs. We have not had them for ever so long, and we must remember and have them again, they are so good. And Brownie, remind me to have chicken for dinner the night before the party, so there will be some to warm up the next day."

"Wait one minute, Mother, please. I want to ask Norah if these are what she had thought of for us."

Strangely enough they were, only she had intended to have the rice shells filled with scrambled eggs. "But the chicken's better," she said. "Trust your mother for thinkin' of it."

Brownie ran back again. "I just wanted to be sure she hadn't thought of anything nicer," she said. "And she hadn't. These are going to be perfectly lovely."

"Now for the potatoes; what kind do you think you would like?"

"I can make nice ones, chopped and fried," said Brownie proudly.

"I don't believe we had better give those small children anything fried, dear; I'm pretty sure their mothers would not like that. What would you think of the potato puff Norah makes out of left-over mashed potato?"

"Just the thing. I wouldn't have to boil the potatoes and peel them and mash them. Left-overs are always *so* convenient!"

"Then we must be sure to have mashed potato for dinner the night before the party, or there won't be any left over," said Mrs. Blair, laughing. "Now, write down this receipt; only remember I am making it small for you; for the family you must take two cups or more of potato, and one egg."

POTATO PUFF

1 cup of mashed potato.
¼ teaspoonful salt.
¼ cup of milk.
½ of a beaten egg.
1 teaspoonful of butter.

Mix the potato with the milk and salt and heat it, beating it well.
Then stir in the butter after warming it till soft, and last the egg.
Put in a small dish and bake in a hot oven till brown.

"I think it would be nice to bake this in one of the small brown earthenware dishes, Brownie; they always look well on the table, and a tin or agate pan wouldn't do at all; you know you must serve it right in the pan you bake it in."

"Isn't it funny, you have one-half an egg in the potato and one-half in the rice patties, Mother. Do you do that on purpose?"

"No, it just happened to be so, but it's an economical thing, Brownie, because eggs are so high now-a-days that one has to remember to use them carefully. The sandwiches come next. What kind do you think would be best?"

"Not cheese, Mother; dolls and children don't eat cheese; I know *that*! And not nut; nor ham; nor hard-boiled egg. I can't think of any kind that would do."

"White bread and brown bread put together, just with plain butter, you know; I think those would be lovely for children."

"So they would; I can make those. And we can cut them out in little, little circles."

"I think you could use an egg cup and press it down hard; that would make little circles."

"Just the thing. Now comes the cocoa, and I can make that all alone; may we use the little after dinner coffee cups to drink it out of? We'll be very careful."

"Well, if you'll be *very* careful indeed," Mother Blair said, hesitating.

"Oh, yes, we'll be just awfully careful. And what about jelly?"

"You can have a glass of jelly out of the closet made over for you in this way:"

MADE-OVER JELLY

A glass of currant jelly warmed in a saucepan till it melts.

1 teaspoonful of granulated gelatine.

½ cup of cold water.

2 tablespoonfuls of boiling water.

Put the gelatine into the cold water, stir it well and let it stand for ten minutes; then stir again and add the boiling water and the hot jelly; stir till it is smooth and strain through a coarse bag into two or more small glasses. Put on ice till firm.

"While the jelly is melting you get the rest of the things ready and then it takes only a moment to put them all together. Norah always has a bag because she washes out and puts away those that the table salt comes in. When you have used it don't forget to wash it out for her, will you, dear?"

"No, Mother. Mildred and I never forget to wash up and put things away ever since she said we couldn't come into the kitchen at all unless we always did that. Do you remember how cross she was?"

"I don't wonder, Brownie. Some day when you have a kitchen of your own you will be cross, too, if little girls come in and use your pots and pans and leave them all sticky and messy."

"Of course I will. It makes me feel real cross now just to think of it. I guess we'd better plan the dessert before I get worse."

"Perhaps we had," laughed Mother Blair. "Those children must have something very simple, indeed, and I really can't think of anything better for them than cornstarch pudding."

"Well," said Brownie doubtfully, "that certainly won't hurt them."

"I know you don't like it very well, and grown people don't care for it either, but it is good for children, and if you learn to make it for them you can easily change the rule a little bit and make it in half a dozen different ways which grown-ups do like. I'll give you two or three rules for your book and you can try them all. Here is the first, for your party:"

PLAIN CORNSTARCH PUDDING

2/3 cup of scalded milk; put in the double boiler.
1½ tablespoonfuls of cornstarch.
½ tablespoonful of sugar.
1 pinch of salt.
2 tablespoonfuls of cold milk.
1 egg.
¼ teaspoonful vanilla.

While the milk is heating till it scalds (that is, till the top wrinkles, but it does not quite boil), mix the cornstarch, sugar and salt in the cold milk and then pour slowly into the scalded milk, stirring well all the time till it grows thick; put on the cover and let it cook eight minutes. Beat the egg without separating it and stir this in and cook one minute; take it off the stove, add the vanilla, pour it into a mold and let it get firm; serve with cream.

"You see that isn't bad at all; but to make it ever so much better try this:"

CHOCOLATE CORNSTARCH PUDDING

Melt a square of unsweetened chocolate by putting it into a saucer over the steam of the tea-kettle; stir this in just before adding the egg. Pour into a pretty mold on ice; turn it out and heap whipped cream around it.

ALMOND CORNSTARCH PUDDING

Use almond flavoring instead of vanilla, and when you take the pudding off the fire, stir in a cup of chopped almonds. Serve with whipped cream.

"That last one sounds, oh, so good, Mother. Can't I make that for Sunday dinner?"

"Yes, indeed you can, and Father will love it, I know. Now, Brownie, let me tell you just one thing more about the dessert for the party; put the pudding into egg cups, and fill them just half full; then you see when you turn them out they will be lovely little molds, one for each child; and you can have the cream in the small silver pitcher to pass with them."

"What a nice party it will be," sighed Brownie. "I'm so glad Helen is only five, because if she were older we couldn't have these cunning, cunning things."

The party really was lovely. The little table had six low seats around it, a hem-stitched lunch cloth over it and a small vase of flowers in the center. The little girls, each with her best doll in her lap, sat around it, too impressed to talk. First they had rice patties filled with hot creamed chicken on little plates, and spoonfuls of brown potato puff; with these the little round sandwiches were passed, brown on one side and white on the other, and tiny cups of cocoa, and helpings from the little glass of jelly which Brownie had turned out in a pretty red mold on a little bit of a glass dish. After they had eaten all they possibly could of these things Norah came in with some more small plates and each one had a little mold of delicious cold pudding, with cream to put on it and two small star-shaped cookies to eat with it. Oh, it was all so good! And the best thing about it was that Brownie really made every single thing they had all by herself, except the cookies. Mildred had made those the day before for her. "I'm so sorry I'm too big to come to the party," she said, "but at least I can make doll-cookies."

"'Doll and little-girl cookies,' you mean," corrected Brownie.

CHAPTER XIV

WHEN NORAH WAS AWAY

One day a messenger boy went around to the kitchen door with a telegram for Norah, telling her that her sister had broken her arm and she must come at once and take care of the children; as there were nine of them, including a tiny baby, Norah felt she must take the very first train, and so in only an hour she was off, and the Blairs' kitchen was empty.

"However, it isn't as though we didn't know how to cook," said Brownie, when she came home from school and found out what had happened. "Every single one of us can cook—even Jack."

"*Even* Jack," called her brother from the dining-room. "I heard that, Brownie Blair, and I'll tell you this: I can cook just as well as any one in this family, if I do say it."

"Prove it, then," laughed his mother, "I got the lunch alone to-day because you were all away; but suppose, instead of having regular dinners while Norah is gone, we have hot suppers, and you three get them without me. Do you think you could manage it? And I will get lunch and breakfast."

"Oh, no, Mother Blair. We will all get breakfast together, and wash the dishes and make the beds before we go to school; we can get up earlier. And every single day we will get supper all alone and you can go out calling or walking or whatever you like."

"Perhaps you'll let me help once in a while," suggested their mother meekly.

"Not once. Of course if you want to make one thing for supper to surprise us some time and have plenty of time to do it while you are getting lunch, we *might* let you do that. A cake, I mean, or gingerbread, just to help out at night; none of us can make many kinds of cake."

"Well, I think most girls know how to make too many kinds of cake and very few kinds of more sensible things, soups and vegetables and so on; and of the two I believe the regular every-day dishes are the more important. You see, you can learn to make cake at any time."

"I think this is a rattling good time for Mildred to learn," declared Jack. "Chocolate layer cake and cocoanut cake and fruit cake are great, and she'll never learn younger, Mother."

"Well, she may make a great big cake for you on Saturday for Sunday night supper, if she wants to; but if she does, I shall expect you to do your share of the cooking every day."

"Emergency cooking is all right; men ought to know how to do that," Jack replied stoutly. "I'm perfectly willing to cook bacon for breakfast, or scramble eggs, or cook fish for supper, or make a stew; anything I cooked in camp I can do with one hand tied behind my back!"

"This is your chance then, to show what you learned last summer. Perhaps if you do splendidly well Father Blair will want to take you again," said his mother. "Now hurry back to school and I will do these dishes and plan the supper and get it all ready for you—on paper,—and then if you want me to, I'll disappear and you may cook it all alone."

"Of course, Mother Blair. Don't you pay any attention to us at all; just come in with Father at half past six and it will be all ready," Mildred said as she hurried away.

That afternoon when the kitchen was all tidy Mother Blair sat down with a pencil and a sheet of paper and wrote out all about the supper. This is what she planned to have, and after each dish she wrote the name of the one who was to make it:

> Cream dried beef (Mildred)
> Corn bread (Jack)
> Cocoa (Brownie)
> Fresh apple-sauce (Mildred)
> Cake (see cake box)

When the three younger Blairs came home and supper time approached, they found this pinned up in the kitchen, and with it the only receipts they needed:

CREAMED DRIED BEEF

1 box of shaved dried beef (or ¼ of a pound if you buy it at the butcher's).
1 tablespoonful butter.
1 tablespoonful flour.
1 cup of hot milk.
2 shakes of pepper.

Cut the beef up into tiny bits; pour boiling water over it and let it stand one minute; pour it off and squeeze the meat dry.

Put the butter in the frying-pan and let it melt; when it bubbles, add the flour and stir till smooth; add the hot milk and pepper, and last the meat; stir till it thickens like cream; serve on squares of hot buttered toast.

"Easy!" said Mildred as she read the receipt over. "Same old white sauce; it's funny how that is used over and over. I think I'll let that wait till just before supper time to make, and get the apple-sauce going. That sounds easy, too."

APPLE SAUCE

6 large, tart apples.
1 cup of sugar.
½ cup water.
¼ teaspoonful cinnamon.

Wipe the apples, cut in quarters, peel and core them. Cut up small and put in a saucepan with the water; cook gently till they are soft, and then add the sugar. When they are transparent and rather smooth they are done; take them up, and either serve as they are, or if you wish, put them through the colander. Sprinkle with cinnamon.

While Mildred was making this, Brownie laid the table, just as she had learned weeks before; then she got out her receipt-book and made the cocoa by that, while Jack made the corn bread by his own camp rule, reciting it aloud as he mixed the different things and shook down the fire and saw that his oven was hot.

"You learn a lot of things camping, Mildred," he said when he finished and cleared up his mixing bowl and other things and wiped off the table. "I never had any idea how careful you had to be to keep things ship shape till I lived with Father up in the woods. He made me clean up after every single thing I made, and wouldn't let me leave a thing around. I thought it was just sort of fussing at first, but after a while I found out it saved time. There weren't half as many dishes to do after a meal, if you cleaned up as you went along, and when you were in an awful hurry to fish or something it helped a lot."

"I know; Mother always tells Brownie and me to do that way. One day we were cooking and I wanted the egg beater; Brownie had used it and left it in the dish pan to soak, so I had to stop and wash it. Then after I used it I put it back in the pan, and Norah needed it and she had to wash it; and that was the way it went all the time till we learned that we must wash up every pot and pan and dish and spoon just the very minute we were through with them. It seems a lot of bother at first but you don't mind after a little. And then, Jack, while we have to wash the dishes at night it will save time to do them as we go along now."

When the toast was made and buttered, Mildred kept it hot while she quickly creamed the dried beef. The cocoa was all ready and so was the brown corn bread, and exactly at half past six o'clock supper was all ready to go right on the table, and everything was as nice as possible. "But then," said Father Blair complacently, "what else can you expect? This corn bread, Jack, tastes to me like that of the good old times."

"And this beef, Mildred, is exactly right, and so is the cocoa."

And so were the apple-sauce and cake, when they came on the table. The cake, especially, seemed particularly good, though it was only the same kind Mildred had often made herself,—the one in her own cook book under the title "Christmas Cake."

"I do think nice cake is just as good as can be," said Mildred, taking a second piece. "I believe I'll learn to make several kinds right away while Norah is gone."

"That's the kind of talk I like to hear," said Jack appreciatively.

In the morning Jack made the fire and started the cereal in plenty of time, while the rest finished dressing. This was the very simple rule he used:

OATMEAL

1 cup of meal.
1 quart of boiling water.
1 teaspoonful salt.

When the water boils hard, add the salt and stir in the meal quickly; put it all into the double boiler and let it cook at least half an hour; take off the cover and let it stand till it gets a little dry (about five minutes). Serve with cream, and, if you like, sliced bananas and a little sugar.

Mother Blair and Mildred laid the table, Brownie got the fruit out of the refrigerator and arranged it and put on the finger-bowls, and then they went into the kitchen to see what should be done next.

"I'm going to cook bacon," announced Jack; "I've got it all ready; you might make the toast, Mildred, and Mother can make the coffee and we'll be all ready in one jiffy."

After breakfast they washed the dishes; or rather Jack washed them and Brownie wiped them, and they laid the lunch table after taking the crumbs up off the floor and table; meanwhile Mother Blair and Mildred made the beds and put the house in order, and when it was time for school everything was done.

"That's easy enough," Jack said as they left. "Rather fun, I think, too. I don't care if Norah stays away quite a while."

For supper that night they found their mother had planned this:

Spanish tomatoes (Mildred)
Stuffed baked potatoes (Brownie)
Biscuits (anybody)
Pancakes and maple syrup (Jack)

"Spanish tomatoes sounds good," said Mildred, reading her easy rule.

SPANISH TOMATOES

6 tomatoes, peeled and chopped, or 1 can.
3 chopped green peppers (first cut each in two and take out the seeds).
½ an onion (chop with the peppers).
¼ teaspoonful salt.
3 shakes pepper.
1 large teaspoonful chopped parsley.

Mix all together and cook about twenty minutes, slowly, or till they look like a thick paste. Pour over buttered toast.

Mother Blair had put a can of tomatoes on the kitchen table and the peppers with it, so it took only a few moments to get this first dish ready; then while it stood waiting to go over the fire and cook, Mildred made the biscuits and popped them into the oven. Brownie washed and baked the potatoes and when they were done she stuffed them beautifully and just browned them at the last moment, and Mildred made the toast to go under the tomatoes.

Everything was delicious, and while Jack made the cakes and brought them in, one plateful after another, all hot and steaming, the family said what fun it all was.

"Isn't it queer that some girls just hate to cook, and think it's simply dreadful when they have no maid and have to do their own work?" said Mildred. "When I'm grown up—I'm going to have a house—no, a flat, I guess, that's cunninger,—and do every single bit of my own work."

"Do," said Brownie enthusiastically; "and I'll come and stay with you and help you."

"So will I," laughed their father.

"And so will I," said Mother Blair. "But you'll have to hurry up and learn lots more, Mildred; there are just hundreds of things you can learn to cook, and all of them are ever so good."

"I'm going to learn every single one," said Mildred solemnly.

As the week went by, the children found they were really learning ever so many of the "hundreds" of good things their mother spoke of. Among them were these, the rules for which they put right in their books with the rest:

EGGS IN RAMEKINS

4 eggs.
4 rounds of buttered toast.
Sprinkle of salt and pepper.

Butter any small dishes; put in the toast rounds, break an egg carefully on each, sprinkle with salt and pepper and bake in the oven till the eggs are done.

EASY MEAT PIE

1 cup chopped cooked meat
1 cup boiling water.
1 teaspoonful chopped parsley.
1 teaspoonful chopped onion.
½ teaspoonful salt.
1 teaspoonful butter.
2 cups mashed potato.

(If the potato is left-over, and so is cold, add ½ a cup of hot milk to it and beat it up till it is smooth and hot.)

Mix the meat, water, and seasoning all together in a saucepan and let it cook till it gets rather dry, stirring it often. Butter a baking dish and cover the sides and bottom with the potato, half an inch thick. Put the meat in the center, and then put the rest of the potato over the top and make it nice and smooth. Put bits of butter all over the top and brown in the oven.

CREAMED SALMON

1 can of salmon (medium size).
1 large cup of white sauce, well seasoned with salt and pepper.

Open the can, drain the fish of oil and take out the skin and bones; mix lightly, lay on squares of buttered toast; put slices of lemon and bits of parsley all around the edge of the platter. (You can use any sort of cooked fish instead of salmon.)

HOT SARDINES

1 box large sardines.
4 slices of toast
Juice of ½ a lemon.
Sprinkles of salt, pepper and dry mustard.

Open the sardines and lift them out carefully; drain the oil off. Put them on a tin plate in the oven to get very hot while you make toast and cut it into strips; cut the crust off and butter them a little. When the sardines are hot put one on each strip of toast, sprinkle with lemon juice, salt, pepper and mustard (only a tiny bit of mustard), and serve at once on a hot dish with parsley all around.

Besides these good things the children made all sorts of potatoes and muffins and everything else they had learned, and they really had a beautiful time. But the most fun of all was on Saturday when they had the cooking to do for two days and plenty of time in which to do it.

CHAPTER XV

THANKSGIVING DAY SUPPER

"Mother Blair, did you ever think that Thanksgiving Day has one great defect?"

"Why, no, Mildred, I don't believe I ever did," smiled her mother. "Do tell me what it is."

"Well, we have to have dinner in the afternoon so the littlest cousins can go home early, and so Norah can get away in time for her regular party—she always goes to one, you know, that evening; and that leaves us with nothing to do for hours before bedtime. I don't know why it is, but that time always drags."

"That is a real defect, Mildred, and I'm glad you told me, because we don't want any part of Thanksgiving Day to drag. It ought to be lovely till the very end. What can you think of that we can do to make it so?"

"I think if all the cousins would stay on instead of going home at dark, and if we arranged something interesting, like a little play or charades, first, and then, when we got hungry, about eight o'clock, we had a hot supper, that would be just perfect."

"Of course! That's a bright idea, Mildred. All the cousins are old enough now to spend the evening, and we can have a lovely time together. You arrange the play, and I'll get up the supper for you."

"No, indeed, Mother Blair! We three juniors will get it—that's part of the fun. And don't you think it would be nice to have it in here on the big library table? We could bring the things in on trays and then just help ourselves."

"That's another bright idea! Of course it would be delightful to have it in here. Then afterwards we could have a wood fire in the grate and sit around it to tell stories, and have games, and charades, and sing some songs together, and be just as thankful as possible. What shall we have for supper? I fancy we shall not want anything very heavy after our dinner."

"No, of course not; but it can be something awfully good. Cold turkey to begin with, and something hot to go with it, and—and what else, Mother Blair?"

"Oh, cranberry jelly, and perhaps a salad, and then something sweet to finish with. Do you think that would do?"

"Yes, and some kind of a hot drink, I suppose; coffee for Father and Uncle and Aunt Mary and you, and cocoa for the rest of us; only I'm so tired of cocoa, I don't believe I could drink a drop."

"We certainly have had it pretty often for lunch lately; I've noticed it myself and meant to speak to Norah about it. I think I can find something else for all of us which you will like better—something especially meant for Thanksgiving."

"What the Pilgrim Fathers had for their Thanksgiving dinner, I suppose," laughed Mildred. "I'm sure it will be good, too, and we'll love it."

School closed the day before Thanksgiving, and that afternoon Mildred and Brownie began to be thankful, because there would be no more lessons till Monday. They put their books away, planned the funny little play they were going to have the next evening, and got together everything they would need for that; then they said it was time to think about the supper in the library.

"We will wait till Norah has gone out and the kitchen is all in order," said Mildred. "Then we can get out the things we want to carry into the other room, and put them on two trays; Jack and Cousin Fred can carry them when we are ready. Plates, and knives, and forks, and glasses, and napkins; and the platter of turkey—"

"And salt," said Brownie, "and bread, and butter."

"Yes; and cranberry jelly. Then we will make the hot things and bring them in afterward."

"What shall we make to-day, Mildred?"

"I wonder if Norah has made the cranberry jelly for dinner yet; if she hasn't, you and I might make that now, and divide it and put part away for the supper. And we can make the dessert, or whatever Mother thinks we had better have. The salad we shall have to make to-morrow."

Norah was that very minute preparing to make the cranberry jelly, but she said she was in a hurry, and the girls could make it if they would promise not to get in her way. They got the receipt from their mother, and began in a corner as far off from Norah as they could get.

CRANBERRY JELLY

1 quart of cranberries. Pick them over and wash them, then chop them a little.

1½ cups of cold water.

2 cups of sugar.

Boil five minutes; rub while hot through a sieve, and pour into a pretty mold.

This rule, of course, had to be doubled for two molds. They found it was not very easy to get the cranberries through the sieve; by talking turns, however, they were slowly squeezing them through when Norah came to their aid and gave them the wooden potato-masher to use instead of the spoon they were working with. The molds were set away to get hard, and then they asked their mother for something else to do.

"I've been thinking," she said, "that we ought to have for supper something the men would like very much; they will have had turkey once already, and perhaps they will be tired of it. Would you like scalloped oysters?"

"Mother, we'd perfectly love them!" exclaimed Mildred. "But do you think we could make them? I always thought they were very hard to make."

"My dear, they are the easiest thing in the world. To save time, you may copy the rule now, and then to-morrow, when everybody is here, I will not have to stop visiting and explain it."

SCALLOPED OYSTERS

1 quart of oysters.

2 packages of crackers, or as many loose ones—about half a pound. Roll fine.

Salt, pepper, and butter.

1 small cup of milk.

Drain the oysters and examine each one carefully to see that it is free from shell; strain and measure the juice; add to it an equal quantity of milk. Butter a deep baking-dish and put in a layer of crumbs, and cover these with a layer of oysters; sprinkle with salt and pepper and dot with butter; put on another layer of crumbs, then one of oysters, season, and so on till the dish is full, with a layer of crumbs on top; cover with small bits of butter; pour on the oyster juice and milk, and bake about half an hour, or till brown. Serve at once—it must not stand.

"Sometimes, instead of baking these in one large dish, I fill little brown baking-dishes in just the same way; only, of course, I do not bake these so long—only ten or fifteen minutes. And sometimes for a lunch party, I get from the fish-market very large oyster, or clam, or scallop shells, and fill those instead of the little dishes, and they are very pretty."

"Mother Blair, those would be sweet—simply sweet! I think I'll give a luncheon and have them."

"Do, Mildred, and I'll help," said Brownie, unselfishly.

"Or you can have a luncheon and *I'll* help!" Mildred replied. "And now what else can we do to-day, Mother? Make some sort of dessert?"

"Yes, I think so; try this; it's simple and very nice."

CHOCOLATE CREAM

1 pint of milk.

4 tablespoonfuls of sugar.

2 squares of unsweetened chocolate.

1 tablespoonful of cornstarch.

1 pinch of salt.

½ teaspoonful of vanilla.

½ pint of thick, sweet cream. (Or this may be omitted.)

Put the milk in a saucepan after taking out a small half-cupful and mixing it with the cornstarch; put in the sugar and salt. Scrape the chocolate (the squares are those marked on the large cake) and put this in next. When it steams and the chocolate is melted and looks brown and smooth, stir up the cornstarch and put it in, stirring till smooth. Cool, add the vanilla, and pour into glasses. Just before serving put a spoonful of whipped cream on top of each glass.

"I do love that," said Brownie, as she wrote down the last word. "When I eat it, I always think I'm eating melted chocolate creams."

"So do I!" laughed Mildred. "Perhaps Uncle Tom and Aunt Mary won't eat their creams to-morrow night, and then you and I can have them for lunch the next day, Brownie."

"They'll surely eat them!" sighed Brownie. "They're too good to leave."

When these were made and safely put away, all but the creamy tops, which were to go on just before supper the next day, Jack came strolling in.

"Smells awfully good!" he said. "Turkey, and onions, and mince-pies, and spicy things. Got any cooking for a boy to do—proper cooking, I mean?"

"I've just thought of something," his mother said quickly, "and I need you to do it right away. The girls are getting up a supper for Thanksgiving night, and they really ought to have some cake to eat with the dessert they have just been making."

"Cake!" ejaculated Jack. "I draw the line at cake, Mother Blair; making cake is not a man's job."

"Not cake, Jack,—only something to go in cake. I want you to crack some nuts and pick them out for the girls. Here is what they are going to make now."

NUT CAKES

2 eggs.
1 cup of light brown sugar.
1 cup of nut meats, chopped fine.
2 tablespoonfuls of sifted flour.
¼ teaspoonful of salt.

Beat the eggs without separating them, and stir in the sugar, flour, and salt. Add the nuts last, and spread the whole in a thin layer on a well-greased tin; bake ten minutes, or till the top is brown. Cut into squares and take quickly from the tin; lay on a platter till cold.

Jack thought he could crack and even pick out nuts without injuring his dignity, so he went to work on a panful of pecans, and, by the time Mildred and Brownie were ready to chop them, they were all ready and waiting. Before long the little cakes were in the oven and out again, crisp and hot; almost too good to be saved, the girls thought, and so did Jack. But they knew there would not be time to-morrow to make any others, so they had to keep these, and when they were cold, shut them up in the cake-box.

"Now I think you have cooked enough for to-day," said their mother, after she had tasted one small crumb of their cakes and pronounced them perfect.

"But, Mother, what about the salad?" asked Brownie.

"Oh, do you really think we need salad with all these good things?"

"Honestly, I don't think we need it at all," said Mildred; "but I do think it would be nice to have it, because it's a party."

"Very well! But what can we have? Lettuce, and tomatoes, and other fresh vegetables are really out of season, or, at any rate, we cannot get them in this town; and yet we ought to have a green salad, because, of course, nobody could possibly eat chicken or lobster salad after a Thanksgiving dinner."

"I could!" called Jack, from the next room; but nobody paid any attention.

"Well, here is an idea—string-bean salad. That is very easy to make, and very good, too, and we can make it out of canned beans and nobody will know it. I will tell you how to make it now, because I'll be so busy to-morrow, and then, in the afternoon, you can get it ready quickly."

STRING-BEAN SALAD

1 pint of string beans, cooked and cold.
2 hard-boiled eggs.
A little lettuce, if you have it.
French dressing.

Drain the beans well and sprinkle them with a little salt and pepper. If they are canned, let them lie on a platter for at least an hour. Arrange them on a few white lettuce leaves on plates, or omit the lettuce and use a few yellow celery leaves; put two strips of hard-boiled egg on the plate, one on each side of the beans, and, just before serving, pour a little French dressing over all. This salad must be very cold.

"Now, certainly, that is all," said Mother Blair, as they wrote this down, "and I'm sure nobody will go home hungry after such a supper as that!"

"And what hot drink are you going to have, Mother?"

"Oh, I almost forgot that. I planned something which is especially Thanksgivingy, too. It is really and truly what the Pilgrim Fathers are supposed to have made for Thanksgiving Day out of wild grapes; but I am sure they had no lemons or spices, so it could not have been quite as good as this. We will have this with the turkey and oysters for the supper, and no coffee or cocoa."

1 quart of bottled grape-juice.

1 pint of water.

1 cup of sugar.

2 lemons.

2 sticks of cinnamon.

1 dozen cloves.

Put the spices in a piece of thin cloth and tie this up like a bag; put it in a saucepan with the grape-juice, sugar, and water, and let it slowly heat till it steams; stir well and let it stand on the back of the fire for ten minutes. Add the juice of the lemons and the thin yellow rind of one (you can peel this off in a strip and drop it in); bring it all to the boiling-point, take out the lemon-peel, taste it, and, if not sweet enough, add more sugar. Serve very hot.

The next evening, just as it grew dark, Mildred and Jack hung a sheet before the double doors of the library, and they, with some of the cousins, gave a funny shadow-play, "Young Lochinvar," with a rocking-horse for the "steed," and a clothes-basket for a boat, and their father read the poem as they acted it. When everybody had stopped laughing at it, the junior Blairs brought in the supper (the oysters had been quietly cooking while they played), and arranged it on the library table. Everything was hot and delicious, or cold and delicious, and the mulled grape-juice was almost the best of all. After everything had been eaten up, they all gathered around the fire and told stories. At last, when the visitors had gone and bedtime had come for the Blairs, Mildred said impressively:

"Now *that* was what I call a Thanksgiving Day without a flaw!"

CHAPTER XVI

CANDY FOR THE FAIR

The Alcott School, which Mildred and Brownie attended, was going to give a Christmas fair. That is, they were going to have a big, beautiful fair to which everybody in town was to go and buy their Christmas presents, and afterward the money was to be given to the children's ward in the new hospital. Mildred and Brownie were on the candy committee, and, of course, they were much excited. They had to have so much candy for a whole town of people that they did not know where it was to come from.

"We could go around and ask for contributions," said Mildred to her mother; "but the trouble is that everybody in the school is doing that very thing, asking and asking and *asking*!"

"You might make a good deal of candy yourselves, and perhaps other people who would not care to buy quantities to give you, would make some too. Home-made candy always sells well."

"Miss Betty makes the loveliest pinoche!" said Brownie, thoughtfully.

"So she does. Suppose we ask her about planning to make candy at home."

Miss Betty had just come in from a meeting of her own committee on the fair, and was as interested as could be in the candy table.

"I'll tell you what to do," she said. "Get as many people as you can to give you just a little money, fifty cents, or even twenty-five, in place of giving you any candy—they will be glad to do that, you see, because it would save them ever so much which they can spend on the fair in other ways. Then we will buy sugar, and nuts, and such things with the money, and get all the girls on your committee to help on the candy-making, either in their own homes—"

"Oh, at our house, Miss Betty," begged Brownie; "that will be a party!"

"Very well, if your mother doesn't mind," laughed Miss Betty. "Then, when we see how much we can make in two afternoons, we will beg enough for the rest that we need. And I'll help you. I make awfully good candy!"

When the girls told their mother the plan, she said, "That's a bright idea!" and told the girls to ask the eight others on the committee to go to work at once and get the money for materials.

The next days were busy ones, and when, three days before the fair, the committee met, they were astonished to see how much money they had collected, enough to buy all the materials and have a good sum over. The girls all promised to help make the candy, and said they would surely be at the Blairs' for two whole afternoons, from two o'clock till dark, beginning the next day.

Jack went down-town and bought everything on the list Miss Betty gave him. White sugar and brown, flavoring, chocolate and nuts, citron and little rose-leaves, pink and green coloring, paraffin paper, and all kinds of boxes, little and big, covered with holly paper, or plain red paper, or just white paper. When he got home; he cracked nuts and picked them out beautifully, nearly all in perfect halves. Miss Betty said he was a regular trump.

The next day, the Blairs had an early lunch, and then Norah put the dining-room and kitchen in order, and got out saucepans, spoons, and egg-beaters. Mildred and Brownie laid lunch-cloths over two small tables in the dining-room, and found scissors and anything else they could think of that would be needed. On the dining-room table, across one end, Jack laid a white marble table-top from an old-fashioned table in the attic, and this they washed off and made very clean. Mother Blair said she was sure some kinds of candy were made on marble, and she meant to be prepared.

When the girls had come and their hands and aprons were ready, Miss Betty said she would take four or five girls into the kitchen to start the candy, and the rest could blanch almonds and get them ready to salt; and when the candy was ready for the finishing touches, she would bring it in and show them what to do with it. So she went off with Mildred and three other girls, and Mother Blair and Brownie went to work with the rest on the almonds. They wanted to have quantities of these because they always sold so well at fairs. This was the rule she used:

SALTED ALMONDS

1 pound of Jordan almonds.
White of one egg.
½ teaspoonful of salt.

Put a cupful of shelled almonds into a saucepan of boiling water, enough to well cover them. Put on a cover and let them stand two minutes; take out one and see if the skin slips off easily in your hand; if not, pour off the water, pour on more that is boiling, and let them stand again. When they are ready, dip out a few at a time and keep the rest under water; slip off the skins and put them in bowls till all are done. Beat the white of the egg till half light, mix with the nuts, and spread them on shallow tins; sprinkle with salt and put them in the oven; stir them every few minutes till they become an even, light brown; then take them out.

Instead of having one pound of almonds, they had ten pounds, so the girls had plenty to do to keep them busy till the candy came in. Meanwhile, Miss Betty was showing them how to make:

COFFEE CANDY

3 tablespoonfuls of ground coffee.
1 small cup of boiling water.
2 cups of sugar.
1 cup of chopped nuts.

Boil the coffee in the water for two minutes; then strain through a very fine sieve. Measure one-half a cupful and mix with the sugar; boil without stirring, till it spins a thread when you hold up a little on a spoon. Then stand the saucepan in another, half full of very cold water, and beat rapidly till it becomes a cream; stir in the nuts, pour into a shallow pan and cool, cut in squares.

Miss Betty had to show the girls how to see candy "spin a thread," because those words, she said, came in so often in all rules for candy. She just lifted a little up on the spoon and tipped it; at first the candy just dropped off, but as it grew thick it fell more slowly, and at last a tiny thread floated off in the air as the syrup dropped.

Of course, they made a great deal of this candy, as it was easy. And when it was cool, they took the pans to the girls in the dining-room. Two of them left the almonds, and cut it up and packed it carefully in boxes which they lined with paraffin paper, tied each one up with narrow ribbon, labeled them with the name, and then put them aside. Meanwhile the girls in the kitchen made:

FONDANT

1 cup of granulated sugar.
½ cup of milk.

Put this on the stove to heat, and stir till the sugar is dissolved, but, until then, do not let it boil. When there is no sugar left on the edges or bottom of the saucepan, let it boil without stirring; have ready a cup of cold water, and after three minutes drop in a little bit and see if you can make it into a ball in your fingers; if not, boil again till you can. Shake the saucepan occasionally so the sugar will not burn. When you can make a firm but not a hard ball, take it off, and set it in a pan of cold water till it is cool enough to put your finger in without burning. Then stir and beat, and, when it begins to get hard, knead it with your hands. Add flavoring while still rather soft.

"This," Miss Betty said to the girls, "is the one thing, above all others, that you must learn to make, because it is the beginning of all sorts of cream candies. In part of it we can put almond flavoring and make it into balls and put a half-almond on top; or use vanilla flavoring, and bits of citron on top. Or we can add chopped nuts to it, or roll pieces of Brazil nuts in, and so on. And of course some of it we will color green, to put green pistachio-nuts on, and pink, to put bits of rose-leaves on. And we can take it while it is still pretty soft, and make little balls of it and dip each one in melted chocolate with the tip of a fork, and make lovely chocolate creams."

"Oh, Miss Betty, let me make those!" begged Mildred; and "Oh, Miss Betty, let me make pistachio creams!"; and "Oh, please, *dear* Miss Betty, let me make the nut creams!" begged the girls. Miss Betty laughed, and shook her head at them all. "The dining-room girls will finish these, all but the chocolate creams—those we will make to-morrow." So she took all the pans of fondant into the dining-room, and Mother Blair showed the girls there how to turn this plain white candy into colored bonbons, working on the marble slab; they were lovely when they were finished, and packed in boxes like the rest. Meanwhile, Miss Betty said they would make:

CHOCOLATE COCOANUT CAKES

1 cup of sugar.
¼ cup of water.
  White of 1 egg.
1 cup of grated cocoanut from a package.
2 squares of chocolate, melted.

Let the sugar and water boil till it spins a thread. Beat the egg white stiff, and very slowly pour in the syrup while beating all the time; add the cocoanut, and then the melted chocolate. Drop on sheets of buttered paper in spoonfuls.

"If you want to have these like little biscuits, do not put in the chocolate; just put them on the paper after spreading it in shallow tins, and bake them till they are brown on top. I think it would be nice to make some of each."

When these were done and carried into the dining-room, Miss Betty said: "And now I will show you how I make my very own pinoche. When I have to earn my living, I shall do it by making this candy, and I'm sure in a very short time I'll be a millionaire." The girls laughed, and said they wanted to learn to get rich too.

PINOCHE

2½ cups of brown sugar.

½ cup of cream.

Butter the size of an egg.

½ cup of chopped walnuts.

½ cup of chopped almonds.

1 teaspoonful of vanilla.

Boil the sugar, cream, and butter together twenty minutes; add the nuts and vanilla, and beat well; when smooth and creamy, pour into buttered tins; when cool, cut in squares.

"It's just as well we have so many to work," said Mildred. "It takes lots of strength to beat this candy."

"Yes, we need Jack's strong arm," said Miss Betty, smiling. "To-morrow, we must get him to help. Now here is another kind of nut candy that is very good indeed, and when you are all done with that pinoche, we will make this next."

NUT CREAMS

3 cups of light brown sugar.

Whites of 2 eggs.

1 cup of boiling water.

1 cup of chopped nuts.

1 teaspoonful of vanilla.

Boil the sugar and water, stirring and beating till the sugar is all dissolved; then let it boil without stirring till it spins a thread. Remove from the fire and let it stand on the table for just a moment, to be sure it has stopped boiling; then pour it over the stiff whites of the eggs, beating with a wire beater all the time; put in the vanilla while you are beating. When it is creamy and getting stiff, add the nuts, stir well, and spread on buttered paper. If you prefer, do not use vanilla, but almond flavoring, and add almonds instead of other nuts.

"Now, girls, just one more kind and that will be enough, I am sure. To-morrow we will change work, and I will teach all this to the other girls while you make salted almonds and tie boxes; I'm sure we shall sell all we can make."

"This Candy ought to be at least a Dollar a Pound."

"This candy will be worth a dollar a pound!" said Mildred.

"At least that," said Miss Betty, laughing; "only we won't ask quite that much, I think. Now this is the last receipt."

CHOCOLATE SQUARES

1 cup of sugar.
¼ cake of chocolate.
½ cup of molasses.
½ cup of milk.
½ cup of butter.

Mix this all together and boil it twenty minutes; cool it a very little and add 1 teaspoonful of vanilla. Pour in pans, and, when cool, mark off in squares.

It was dark when all this candy was done and in the boxes. The girls were tired, but delighted with their work, and the next day they came, eager to finish it. Those who worked in the kitchen made the same things as the other girls had made before, and, when everybody was done, it was astonishing how many, many boxes they had.

They had already decided not to have any two-pound or five-pound boxes, but to make only pound and half-pound ones, as these would sell better. They tied up the boxes which were covered with holly paper with red ribbons, and the red boxes with holly ribbons, and the plain white boxes with red, with a bit of holly tied in each bow. When Norah saw them all, she said they were "stylish." Certainly they were pretty, and the candy was delicious, and fresh as well, and all the committee and Mother Blair and Miss Betty were just as proud as proud could be.

Selling Candy at the Christmas Fair

When the fair was over, the ladies who were in charge of it sent a special little note to the candy committee telling them how well they had done.

"Next time we will make ever so many more kinds of candy," said Mildred, as they talked it all over. "I never knew there were so many. I used to think all you could make at home were molasses candy and peanut brittle, and everybody can make those, so they are not much fun."

"When the children get into their ward, we will make some candy for them," said Brownie. "I think the children with broken legs, and bad knees, and the not-very-sick children would like some, especially if we put it in white boxes and tie them up with big bows of ribbon."

"Of course they would," said Mildred. "It would be just lovely and would help them to get well ever so much quicker, I know.

CHAPTER XVII

EXAMINATION DAY

"Children," said Mother Blair on New Year's day, "when you have all finished whatever you are doing and have a whole hour to spare, I want you to bring your receipt books into the sitting-room. I'm going to have an examination."

Jack gave a loud groan.

"That's no fair, Mother. No exams in vacation!"

"Yes, it is fair, perfectly fair to have this examination in vacation time, because you never have a moment while school is going on to give me for it; now is my only chance. But it won't be a very long or severe one. I fancy I can find out all *you* know about cooking in a very short time, Jack!"

Jack laughed and went upstairs for his book, and presently they all gathered in the sitting-room by the fire. The three children sat in a row on the great big sofa with the pillows tucked behind them, and Mother Blair sat in front, exactly like a teacher. She had three pads and pencils ready, and three packages well wrapped up, in her lap.

"It was just a year ago to-day that we got those books," said Brownie. "Mine has heaps of rules in it, too."

"So has mine," said Mildred, turning the leaves. "I did not know I had so many. And what fun we had making some of the things! Do you remember your cheese dreams at the House-in-the-Woods party, Jack? And the Hallowe'en things in the chafing-dish? And the attic picnic, Brownie? I'm sorry we can't have all those parties over again, Mother."

"We'll have plenty more, dear, and better ones, too. But how many receipts have you, Jack?"

Jack proudly displayed his camping receipts and a few others, principally chafing-dish rules. "Lots!" he said.

"Not half enough. You've done only pretty well, Jack; but a beginning is something, after all. But now, children, the examination is going to begin. Here is a written question for each of you, and you are to write the answer down on this pad."

"Dreadful," murmured Mildred, accepting her slip of paper and pad with a long sigh. This is what she read:

"What would you have for luncheon, if you found in the refrigerator some eggs, a little celery, cold boiled potatoes, a bottle of milk and butter; and beside had in the house cookies and a basket of very poor pears? Look up the rule for each dish in your receipt book."

"That's easy," said Mildred, happily, going to work at once.

Brownie's slip said:

"If you were ordering breakfast to-morrow morning, what would be the nicest things you could think of? And could you make them all?"

And when Jack opened his folded paper he read:

"Plan a Sunday night supper with nothing but what you can make yourself."

"Ask me a hard one," Jack said, waving his paper around his head.

Mother Blair took a book and began to read to herself while the pencils scratched away on the pads and the receipt books were consulted over and over. It was only a few moments before, "Done!" said Mildred, and "Done!" said Brownie. Jack was a trifle slower, and they had to wait for him to finish. It was not so easy an examination as he had thought at first.

"Read the question first and then the answer; you begin, Mildred," said Mother Blair. So Mildred read her question, and then taking her pad read what she had put down:

"For luncheon I would have first, cream of celery soup, made by the rule I copied under cream soups; I learned how to make those when Mother was sick. After that I would have creamed eggs on toast. (You know I can make those, Mother; I made them just last week.) And with them I'd have hashed brown potatoes; that rule I know by heart. And then for dessert I'd stew those poor pears, like apple sauce, you know, only I wouldn't cut them up but keep them in halves the way Norah does; and I'd have the cookies with them."

"Good, Mildred—splendid! I did not know you could manage so well Now let's see what Brownie would have for breakfast."

"Cereal first; see the rule of cereal with dates,—only I'd leave out the dates this time—and then I'd have muffins; of course, I can make those. And coffee, and poached eggs. Do you think that is a good breakfast, Mother?"

"Delicious, dear. I only wish it were breakfast time now. And how did you get along, Jack?"

"You gave me the hardest of all," Jack grumbled. "But I did it, all the same. I'd have cheese dreams, and corned beef hash first; then I'd have pigs in blankets on toast; and camp coffee; and then corn cakes and syrup to finish off with."

Jack smiled complacently. "That's what I call a good, substantial meal."

Mildred was screaming with laughter as he finished.

"Cheese dreams and pigs in blankets, and corned beef hash, Mother Blair! For Sunday night supper!"

"You'd have regular Hallowe'en nightmares after that meal, Jack!" said his mother, laughing too. "However, as you know how to make all those, we will let you have them—on paper. Only when you get a supper for this family you need not have quite so many things, especially if we have company; they might not appreciate them. Now are you ready for the next question?"

The examination proved such fun that they kept it up all the morning. They told how to lay a table for breakfast, luncheon and dinner; how to arrange a sick-room tray; what to give a little child who came in to a meal; how to make fudge, and sandwiches, and tea and salads and cake; how to put up jelly, and how to cook eggs in different ways; some of these things Brownie and Jack did not know, but most of them they wrote down on their papers very well indeed. And they planned all sorts of meals, and that was the most fun of all, family dinners, and company luncheons, and picnic suppers, and party meals for Thanksgiving and Fourth of July and Washington's Birthday and other times. It really was not so much of an examination as it was a game.

Finally Mother Blair said they had done enough. "You know so much more than I thought you did that I'm satisfied," she said. "Really and truly, children, I'm proud of you! You all get a hundred in your examination, and you each have earned a prize beside for standing at the top of your three classes."

Then she opened the packages she had had in her lap all this time and brought out three books.

"Before I distribute the prizes I must make a speech," she said. "That's the way it's always done at school, you know.

"Children: You have done so well in your cooking lessons that I am going to give each of you a real cook book, for you know now how to use one. There are many other dishes beside those you have learned already that I am sure you will want to know how to make, too. All you have to do is to turn to any rule here and follow it carefully, exactly as you do in the books you have made yourselves. Mildred, here is your book— I present it with pride! It's a regular grown-up cook book, only it's a very easy one. And, Brownie, yours is a little girl's cook book; you will love it, and I present it with pride, too, my dear child! And Jack—"

"I do hope mine has plenty of cake in it, Mother, and lovely desserts all made with gelatine, and fancy salads with fixings on them; you know those are the things I really like to make," said Jack demurely.

"I'm sorry to disappoint you," laughed his mother, "but yours is a regular boy's cook book, all about—"

"Camping!" interrupted Jack, as he saw its title. "Well, now, that's about the right kind of a book for me, after all. Say, Mother Blair, I think your prizes are great."

"So do I," murmured Mildred, who was deep in a rule for a perfectly delicious dessert with whipped cream and nuts in it.

But Brownie did not say a word. She was reading the story in her book about how some children learned to cook.

CPSIA information can be obtained
at www.ICGtesting.com
Printed in the USA
LVHW010255200423
744807LV00009B/258

9 781805 474319